NOAH'S
ARK
KNITS

Mo Smith

NOAH'S ARK KNITS

AUTUMN
HOUSE

AUTUMN HOUSE
GRANTHAM ENGLAND

Dedication

*This book is dedicated to
Sandie Manning, my very special friend
and to my Mother, Kathleen Francis,
for all her hard work in helping me
with the knitting of the sweaters*

*The bear that appears in this book is Jed, from
'Teddy Bear Knits' by Mo Smith. The profits
from the sale of this Merrythought bear go to
ACET (AIDS Care, Education and Training)*

EDITORIAL
Tania Kazozi and Paul Dicken

PHOTOGRAPHY
Barrie Davis, Dawson Strange Photography Ltd.

MODELS
Jake Clifford, Faye Thomson, Nathan Erasmus,
Rebekah Coveney, Sam O'Donnell, Anne Ball,
Alex Kazozi, Rebecca Shuai, Rozanne and
Joel van Rensburg

PUBLISHED BY
Autumn House
Alma Park, Grantham, Lincs
England, NG31 9SL

COPYRIGHT
© 1993 by Autumn House

Story and design of garments copyright
© 1993 Mo Smith

Printed in England

British Library Cataloguing in Publication Data
Smith, Mo
  Noah's Ark Knits: 12 Original Sweaters
Illustrating a Story Based on Noah's Ark
for Children and Adults
  I. Title II. Kazozi, Tania
III. Dicken, Paul
646.4
ISBN 1 873796 20 X

Noah's Notes

'Noah's Ark Knits' is Mo's second book which combines an exciting story with sweaters depicting your favourite animals. The story relates the adventures of Majestic the lion on his journey to find Noah's Ark. The story is based on the account of Noah's Ark from the Bible, and the origin of the rainbow, which illustrates God's love to each one of us. I hope you enjoy reading the story as well as knitting your favourite sweater.

The designs range from a 22in (56cm) to a 44in (112cm), using the same graph for all sizes. There are sweaters and cardigans to choose from, knitted in a variety of Double Knitting, Cotton, Chunky and Mohair yarns. Each pattern is star-rated to help you choose the sweater suited to your knitting ability. The instructions are given clearly for each design, using either PATTERN A or PATTERN B for the basic number of stitches, etc. The designs combine the use of embroidery, ribbon and attachments to give your sweater that added dimension and original look.

This book includes:
- Easy-to-follow tables for yarn quantities.
- Easy-to-follow tables for sweater measurements.
- Sections on 'Working with Colours', 'Working from Charts', and 'Embroidery', all to help your sweater have that professional look.
- All the yarn recommended is readily available from your local Sirdar stockist or, alternatively, in kit form from Mo (see Noah's Address Book on page 71).
- The fun buttons are available from Peapods to Zebras (see Noah's Address Book).

P.S.
I hope you have as much fun making and wearing the sweaters as Mo had designing them.

Contents

Majestic's Calling

The sun's rays broke through the tall trees, lighting the winding path through the forest. A lion by the name of Majestic was prowling the undergrowth looking for his evening meal. He was known as the king of the jungle, the bravest of all the animals that lived in his part of the world. Majestic stopped in his tracks as a long, loud roll of thunder echoed across the sky above him. He felt as if someone was speaking to him and he pricked his ears to listen carefully. When the thunder finished Majestic ran to his lioness, Destiny. Excited by what he had heard, he began talking about the long journey he had been told to make. Together they said goodbye to their friends in the forest and headed towards the rocks on the edge of the jungle. When they reached them, Majestic leapt to the top. Looking down over the river he gave a mighty roar. He knew they had a long way to travel and that it would be a long time before they returned to their homeland. They roared a final goodbye as they set off towards the river in the valley below.

The Monkeys' Mischief

The elephants were plodding along extra slowly, which was very frustrating for the lions who were used to racing everywhere. At sunset they arrived at a water hole and settled down for the night. They were beginning to doze off when a thump on Majestic's head woke him with a start. A banana skin had landed directly on the lion's head and as he looked up he saw two monkeys swinging by their tails. Majestic raised his gigantic paw to frighten them away but the monkeys, who were called Mimi and Chieftain, swung from one branch to another, laughing at him. Then Chieftain began to speak to Majestic, saying, 'We have heard that a long way away, beyond the forest, an enormous ark is being built. God told a man called Noah that the earth was going to flood. We know that animals are heading there from all directions. Are you going too?' Majestic, who was really pleased, knew that they were heading for the ark. 'Yes, we are going,' said Majestic. 'Would you like to join us?' Mimi and Chieftain were thrilled to have been asked and all six settled down for the night, looking forward to the morning.

Through the Cornfield

At sunrise the lions, elephants and monkeys set off on the next stage of their journey. From time to time Majestic would run ahead and spy out the land and then rush back to tell the others what to expect. When they were passing through a bright yellow cornfield they heard a peculiar 'oink, oink' sound close by. There in the corner of the field were two pigs, nicknamed Pop and Corn because they were forever tucking into the ears of corn. They came snuffling towards the procession of animals, grunting with curiosity. Pop and Corn didn't seem afraid of the lions or the elephants, but Destiny took an instant dislike to the smell that came with the pigs! She insisted that they went first to the river to have a good wash, and Ellie thought that was a brilliant idea and offered to give them a hand (or rather, a trunk!). It was wonderful to see the pigs splashing in the water, the elephants spraying them with their trunks, the monkeys swinging from one side of the bank to the other, and the lions not daring to get too close just in case Alf and Ellie soaked *them* again!

Building the Ark

As the journey continued, Majestic learnt more about Noah and the ark from Mimi and Chieftain. He heard that God was really hurt by the awful things that people were doing, and he told Noah to build an ark. It was to be over a hundred metres long, 23 metres wide, and 14 metres high, with a roof set in place on top. God told Noah to give the ark three decks divided into rooms so that Noah, his family and at least two of every animal, bird and insect would be safe when the flood came. Majestic thought for a while as he pictured the enormous ark filled with creatures of every kind. Chieftain told him of the rumours he had heard back in the jungle about Noah's friends who were laughing at him and not listening to his warning. As they were all travelling along together, Majestic saw two horses grazing in a field. They were strong and beautiful and as Majestic approached them they raced round the field, their heads held high, rearing and bucking as they went. The horses, who were called Firecrest and Flame, had heard whispers from the other animals that something terrible was about to happen and they had become very restless. Both horses whinnied loudly when Majestic asked them to join the other animals on their journey. They raced round the field, jumping the hedge and only just missing Pop and Corn on the other side!

The Cat and Mouse Game

In one corner of a nearby field was a large haystack where two mice called Bubble and Squeak were frantically trying to escape the claws of two rather unpleasant cats, Weazle and Pickles. When Majestic appeared from behind a bale of hay he was the biggest cat any of them had ever seen! Weazle arched his back and hissed loudly, making his fur stand on end. But the lion spoke gently to them all, and because his breath was warm and friendly Pickles liked him at once. They all began to chase each other round the bales until Alf appeared suddenly and Bubble and Squeak jumped between Majestic's legs for safety. Weazle and Pickles darted over a nearby fence to escape. When they peeped over to see what was going on they saw the procession of animals stretching into the distance. Right at the back they saw that Bubble and Squeak had joined the line. Weazle decided to follow, and look for another chance to catch their prey! Majestic, who guessed what they were thinking, roared a warning at them. Not wanting to be left behind, the cats thought better of it and followed meekly behind the rest.

The Big Splash

A few miles further on the procession arrived at a stone bridge which crossed a fast-flowing stream. Alf and Ellie led the way with Mimi and Chieftain darting between their legs. The others all decided on this occasion not to get their feet wet! Firecrest and Flame trotted over the bridge with their heads held high, listening to the sound of their hooves on the stones beneath them. When Weazle and Pickles were half-way across, Pickles spotted a frog sitting on the wall and leapt forward to catch him.

Fortunately, Freddie the frog saw the danger and hopped over to the grass. He landed on a toadstool where his mate Freda was sitting. But Pickles wasn't so lucky. She didn't manage to stop in time and toppled over the wall into the water beneath. It is well known that cats hate water, but the fuss Pickles made was totally over the top. The water was only a few inches deep, but that was a few inches too many for Pickles! She struggled to the bank where she saw the frogs hopping up and down with laughter. Feeling ashamed, Pickles slunk, tail down low, to her place at the back of the procession, but Majestic asked her to go back and invite Freddie and Freda to join them on their journey. She was not very happy about doing this, but the frogs were delighted to accept.

They were told the exciting news about Noah and the ark as they hopped along.

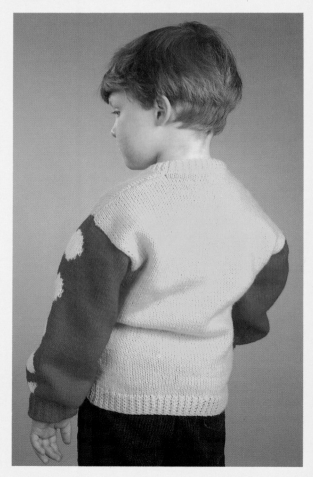

Over the Mountains

When everyone was safely over the bridge, Majestic began to sing quietly to himself. He knew their destination was still a long way off, and he was getting very tired, but he also knew time was short and they must keep going. It wasn't long before they reached the woods at the bottom of the mountains and there, under a tall fir tree, were two cuddly-looking bears, one named Cuddles and the other Jed. The bears offered to guide Majestic and all his friends over the mountains. The lion roared happily as the two bears explained that they knew Noah was building an ark to carry every kind of creature on the earth. They would be so pleased to guide the procession over the mountains. Majestic wasn't sure, thinking of the dangers that lay ahead of them, but Jed and Cuddles took their place at the front of the line and together they started to lead the animals through the most difficult part of their journey. When they reached the top the view was breathtaking, and they all thanked God for the bears who had guided them so well.

The Skating Rink

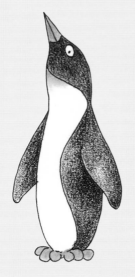

Along the way every kind of animal you could think of joined them, and when they were all talking at the same time the sound was quite deafening! Sometimes, as they remembered their families back home, one or two of them would feel homesick. Ellie tried to cheer them up by teaching them a special rhyme which went like this:

Together we will travel
Through forest, field and land,
Looking to our Maker
To lead us by His hand.

We know He's always with us
Watching from above,
He'll guide us on our journey
And protect us with His love.

On the far side of the mountain Majestic saw snow for the very first time, and in the distance he could see a frozen lake with two penguins walking on the ice! When the procession began to walk over the lake they slipped and slid all over the place. To everyone's surprise the lions and cats had a great time, even though their paws were frozen!

The Great Arrival

The penguins, called Sam and Pippa, joined the long trail of animals, and before long they all settled down for the night. In the morning there was great excitement, and Majestic had a feeling that their journey was nearing its end. As they reached the top of a long steep hill, he saw the enormous ark in the valley below. The cry 'we've arrived!' echoed down the line, and Majestic proudly led them all down the hill. Noah came running towards them and flung his arms round Majestic's neck. The lion licked Noah's hands, which were hard and worn from building the ark. As they stood together, other animals began arriving from every direction, many of whom Majestic had never seen before. Noah and his family led them, two by two, up the huge ramp, and each pair were given a special place in the ark. The elephants and other heavy creatures stayed on the lower deck. Weazle and Pickles were placed on the middle deck along with many that they wouldn't usually get along with. Mimi and Chieftain swung their way to the top deck. All the animals from the procession found their special places, and many other creatures, including ladybirds, spiders, snails and tortoises were right at the end. When they were all safely on board the huge ramp was raised and the whisper went round the ark that the Lord had shut them in.

Ship Ahoy!

All was quiet and the rain began to fall. It became heavier and heavier and the water flooded the earth. It swirled round the ark and the ark began to float. All the animals kept very quiet, a little frightened by what was happening to them. Some of the animals cried for their friends they had left behind. Destiny saw how they were feeling and began to sing to them. It wasn't long before they all joined in. Sometimes grumbles came to Noah's ears — from the mice who were fed up with being chased by the cats, from the dogs who couldn't bear the smell of the skunks, from the seals who longed for a swim, and from the hedgehogs who were tired of being told they were pricking everyone else! Noah helped where he could, and moved a few of them around. This stopped the grumbles. It rained for forty days and forty nights without stopping, and the water covered the earth for 150 days. All through that time no one went hungry or thirsty, and Noah's family worked very hard to keep them all happy.

One day, after the rain had stopped, Noah opened a window and sent a raven out to see if there was any land, but he returned with the news that the earth was still covered with water. Noah, his family and all the animals, continued their voyage. They all looked forward to the day when the water would disappear.

The Glorious Rainbow

Later, Noah released a dove, but he too returned exhausted to the ark, not having found anywhere to land. A week passed and Noah sent the dove out again. This time he brought back an olive leaf in his beak. At last the water was going down. When Noah sent the dove out again he didn't return. The ark came to rest on the top of a mountain and at long last the huge ramp was lowered. With great excitement Majestic and Destiny, Alf and Ellie, Mimi and Chieftain, Pop and Corn, Firecrest and Flame, Weazle and Pickles, Bubble and Squeak, Freddie and Freda, Jed and Cuddles, Sam and Pippa, and all the other creatures, began making their way to the dry land. Majestic and Destiny thanked Noah for all that he had done, and Noah told them that God would never flood the earth again. While they were all looking towards the sky a light shower of rain fell, and the most beautiful band of colour curved from one side of the sky to the other. The colours red, orange, yellow, green, blue, indigo and violet all merged together to form the first rainbow. It told Majestic and Destiny that God loved His creation so much. They ran and leapt across the plains, enjoying the feel of the earth beneath their paws again. Some time later Destiny gave birth to three cubs, and just as the last one was born there was a short shower of rain. Majestic looked up and there was the rainbow, with its glorious colour reminding them that God would always keep His promise never to destroy the earth again by flood.

Working Notes

WORKING WITH COLOURS

There are two methods of working with colours recommended in the patterns in this book. The first is for repeated patterns, when the contrast colour can be stranded across the back of the work. For best results place the contrast colour over the background colour every three stitches, without holding it too tightly. If you hold the yarn you are carrying across too tightly puckering will occur. If you have worked stranding correctly the yarns will be running evenly across the back of the work at the same tension as the knitting.

The second method is recommended for all motifs. To help different yarns separate when working complicated colour patterns, wind manageable lengths on to bobbins (available in most wool and haberdashery shops), yarn holders or spools. When changing colour, join new colour in by tying a half knot and work across stitches. Repeat again when necessary (this includes the background colour). On all subsequent rows lay the last colour used over the next, pick up the colour to be used and continue working. This avoids a hole appearing between different colours. Each colour is therefore carried up the work and not across the back. This gives a much better finish to the work. When you are sewing off the ends, thread your needle and holding it at the back of the work, with right side facing, pull the needle to see which way it is best to sew the end off. Sew securely down, making sure it doesn't show through on the right side.

WORKING FROM CHARTS

On the graphed patterns each square represents one stitch. The charts are read from the bottom of the chart upwards and from right to left on the first and all odd-numbered rows and from left to right on the second and all even-numbered rows. Therefore the bottom right-hand corner indicates the first stitch of the graph, knitting from right to left and purling from left to right.

In some of the patterns where the same chart is worked on the Back as well as the Front, the chart is still worked in the same way, but purling from right to left and knitting from left to right. This is clearly indicated in each pattern where necessary.

EMBROIDERY

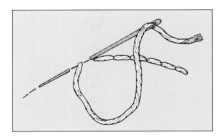

BACK STITCH
Work in small, even stitches by first making a stitch forwards and then a stitch backwards.

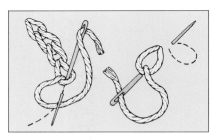

CHAIN STITCH
Loop the working thread under the top of your needle and hold it down with your left thumb while you pick up some of the ground fabric in each stitch. The needle is inserted into the same hole from which it has emerged. To make a leaf shape bring out your needle and insert it into the same spot, bringing it out with a loop under the needle. Take it over the loop so that you make a small tying stitch to anchor it.

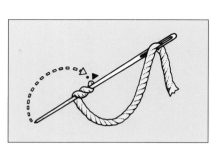

FRENCH KNOT
Holding thread down with the left thumb, encircle thread twice with needle. Then twist needle back to arrow and insert it close to starting point. Pull through to back before repositioning for next stitch.

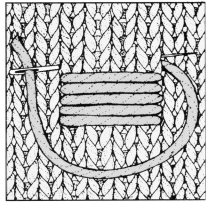

SATIN STITCH
For best results work horizontal straight stitches. The stitches should fit closely together, giving a very smooth surface and straight outside edges.

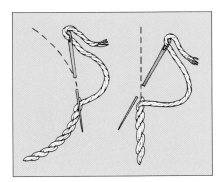

STEM STITCH
Work the stitch with the thread kept on the same side of the needle. For a wider effect insert the needle into the ground fabric at a slight angle. The greater the angle the wider the effect.

LION'S EYE
Outline in
Terracotta

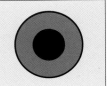

ELEPHANT'S
EYE
Outline in
White

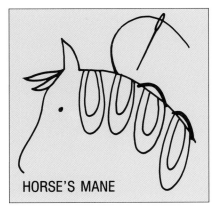

HORSE'S MANE

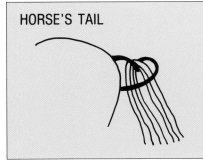

HORSE'S TAIL

FROG'S EYE
Outline in
Black

MONKEY'S
EYE
Outline in
Black

PIG'S EYE
Outline in
Dark Grey

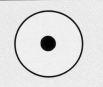

TEDDY'S EYE
Outline in
White

TO MAKE A POM-POM
Cut two ¾in (2cm) circles out of cardboard, cutting a hole ¼in (5cm) in diameter in the centre. Place the two circles together, thread a darning needle with a long length of yarn and wind the yarn round the circles until the hole in the centre is full. Using pointed scissors, cut round the outside of the circle between the two pieces of cardboard and then tie a double length of yarn tightly round the middle. Leave a length to sew on to the sweater in the appropriate place. Trim the pom-pom to the size required (see diagram).

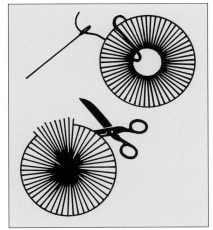

ATTACHING SAFETY EYES
Place the eye through the knitting, then push the backing firmly in place. Once the backing is secure, it is permanent. Make sure that it is in the correct place before fixing the backing on.

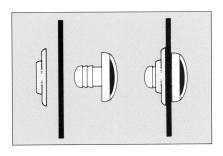

33

Materials

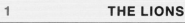

1 THE LIONS

Sirdar Country Style Double Knitting x 50g balls (approx.)

SHADE	KEY	INCH 22 / CM 56	(24 / (61	26 / 66	28 / 71	30 / 76	32 / 81	34 / 86	36 / 91	38 / 96	40 / 102	42 / 107	44) / 112)
(419) Tartan Green	A	1	(1	1	1	2	2	3	3	3	3	3	3)
(489) Pastel Jade	B	1	(1	2	2	2	2	2	2	2	3	3	3)
(425) Golden Sand	C	1	(1	1	1	1	1	1	1	1	1	1	1)
(453) Terracotta	D					...... Small quantity							
(429) Lupin	E	3	(3	3	3	4	4	4	5	5	5	5	5)
(460) Corona Yellow	F					...... Small quantity							
(412) White	G					...... Small quantity							
(417) Black (Embroidery)						...... Oddment							

1 pair 9mm safety Teddy eyes.
Small quantity of washable stuffing.
1 pair No. 3¼mm (UK 10, US 3) needles, 1 pair No. 4mm (UK 8, US 5) needles.
2 stitch holders.

2 THE ELEPHANTS

Sirdar Wash 'n' Wear Double Crepe x 50g balls (approx.)

SHADE	KEY	INCH 22 / CM 56	(24 / (61	26 / 66	28 / 71	30 / 76	32 / 81	34 / 86	36 / 91	38 / 96	40 / 102	42 / 107	44) / 112)
(284) Citron	A	6	(6	7	7	8	8	10	11	12	12	13	13)
(269) Electric Blue	B	1	(1	1	1	1	1	1	1	1	1	1	1)
(278) Cherry	C	1	(1	1	1	1	1	1	1	1	1	1	1)
(251) White	D	1	(1	1	1	1	1	1	1	1	1	1	1)
(238) Silver Blue	E	1	(1	1	1	1	1	1	1	1	1	1	1)
(225) Romantic Pink	F					...... Small quantity							
(275) Black (Embroidery)						...... Oddment							

10in (25cm) of 15mm poppy Offray Singleface Satin ribbon (No. 235).
6in (15cm) of 23mm electric blue Offray Singleface Satin ribbon (No. 352).
2in (5cm) of 7mm white Offray Singleface Satin ribbon (No. 029).
8 red elephant buttons from Peapods to Zebras (address in Noah's Address Book on page 71) — child's.
10 elephant buttons — adult.
1 pair No. 3¼mm (UK 10, US 3) needles, 1 pair No. 4mm (UK 8, US 5) needles.
1 stitch holder.
2 safety pins.

3 THE MONKEYS

Sirdar Country Style Double Knitting x 50g balls (approx.)

SHADE	KEY	INCH 22 / CM 56	(24 / (61	26 / 66	28 / 71	30 / 76	32 / 81	34 / 86	36 / 91	38 / 96	40 / 102	42 / 107	44) / 112)
(411) Cream	A	3	(4	4	5	5	6	6	7	7	8	8	8)
(482) Majestic Mink	B	1	(1	1	1	1	1	2	2	2	2	2	2)
(479) Emerald	C	1	(1	1	1	1	1	1	1	1	1	1	1)
(417) Black	D	1	(1	1	1	1	1	1	1	1	1	1	1)
(477) Indian Yellow	E	1	(1	1	1	1	1	1	1	1	1	1	1)
(425) Golden Sand	F	1	(1	1	1	1	1	1	1	1	1	1	1)
(412) Parasol Pink	G					...... Oddment							
(420) Lobelia	H					...... Oddment							
(449) Royal	J					...... Oddment							
(495) Guard's Red (Embroidery)						...... Oddment							
(412) White (Embroidery)						...... Oddment							

1 pair No. 3¼mm (US 10, US 3) needles, 1 pair No. 4mm (UK 8, US 5) needles.
2 stitch holders.

4 THE PIGS

Sirdar Soft Cotton Double Knitting x 50g balls (approx.)
or alternatively Sirdar Country Style Double Knitting x 50g balls (approx.)

SHADE	KEY	INCH 22 / CM 56	(24 / (61	26 / 66	28 / 71	30 / 76	32 / 81	34 / 86	36 / 91	38 / 96	40 / 102	42 / 107	44) / 112)
(640) Navy	A	6	(6	7	8	9	11	12	13	14	15	15	16)
(441) Light Navy (CS)*		4	(5	5	6	6	7	7	8	9	10	10	10)
(659) Fusia	B	1	(1	1	1	1	1	1	1	1	1	1	1)
(488) Mexican Rose (CS)*		1	(1	1	1	1	1	1	1	1	1	1	1)
(647) Marine Blue	C	1	(1	1	1	1	1	1	1	1	1	1	1)
(420) Lobelia (CS)*		1	(1	1	1	1	1	1	1	1	1	1	1)
(642) Parisian Pink	D	1	(1	1	1	1	1	1	1	1	1	1	1)
(413) Parasol Pink (CS)*		1	(1	1	1	1	1	1	1	1	1	1	1)
Dark Grey (Embroidery)						...... Oddment							

* (CS) = Sirdar Country Style D.K.
20in (51cm) of 39mm Offray Giant Dots ribbon comb. 13.
6in (15cm) of 23mm Offray Confetti Dot Singleface Satin ribbon (Multi).
5in (13cm) of 12mm Offray Confetti Dot Singleface Satin ribbon (Multi).
11in (28cm) of 9mm Offray blue mist Singleface Satin ribbon (311).
3in (7cm) of 7mm Offray electric blue Singleface Satin ribbon (352).
2 white and 2 silver pearls.
8 pink pig buttons from Peapods to Zebras (address in Noah's Address Book on page 71) — child's.
10 pink pig buttons — adult.
1 pair No. 3¼mm (UK 10, US 3) needles, 1 pair No. 4mm (UK 8, US 5) needles.
1 stitch holder.
2 safety pins.

5 THE HORSES

Sirdar Country Style Double Knitting x 50g balls (approx.)

SHADE	KEY	INCH 24 / CM 61	(26 / (66	28 / 71	30 / 76	32 / 81	34 / 86	36 / 91	38 / 96	40 / 102	42 / 107	44) / 112)
(479) Emerald	A	3	(3	3	4	4	4	5	5	5	6	6)
(404) Parchment	B	1	(1	1	1	1	1	1	1	1	1	1)
(417) Black	C				...... Oddment							
(412) White	D	1	(1	1	1	1	1	1	1	1	1	1)
(477) Indian Yellow	E	1	(1	1	1	1	1	1	1	1	1	1)
(439) Dark Chocolate	F				...... Oddment							
(419) Tartan Green	G	1	(1	1	1	1	1	1	1	1	1	1)
(440) Saxe	H	3	(3	3	4	4	4	5	5	5	6	6)
(472) Stormcloud	J				...... Small quantity							
(408) Greystone (Embroidery)					...... Oddment							

Approximately 5g white Mohair (for mane and tail).
1 pair No. 3¼mm (UK 10, US 3) needles, 1 pair No. 4mm (UK 8, US 5) needles.
2 stitch holders.

6 THE CATS

Sirdar Country Style Double Knitting x 50g balls (approx.) for Child's 22-32in (56-81cm)

Sirdar Country Style Chunky x 100g balls (approx.) for Adults's 34-44in (86-112cm)

SHADE	KEY	INCH 22 / CM 56	(24 / (61	26 / 66	28 / 71	30 / 76	32 / 81	34 / 86	36 / 91	38 / 96	40 / 102	42 / 107	44) / 112)
(489) Pastel Jade	A	1	(1	2	2	2	2	3	3	4	4	4	4)
(493) Cardinal	B	1	(1	1	1	1	1	1	1	1	1	1	1)
(404) Parchment	C	1	(1	1	1	1	1	1	1	1	1	1	1)
(440) Saxe	D	3	(4	4	4	5	5	4	4	4	5	5	5)
(460) Corona Yellow (Embroidery) (DK)							Oddment						
(449) Royal (Embroidery) (DK)							Oddment						
(495) Guard's Red (Embroidery) (DK)							Oddment						
(417) Black (Embroidery) (DK)							Oddment						
(412) White (Embroidery) (DK)							Oddment						
(419) Tartan Green (Embroidery) (DK)							Oddment						

5 x 4in (13 x 10cm) piece of black and 5 x 4in (13 x 10cm) piece of white fur fabric.
2 pairs 12mm safety cat's eyes.
1 15mm black and 1 15mm pink safety cat's noses.
6 black and 6 white whiskers.
2 small silver bells.
5in (10cm) of 7mm Offray red Singleface Satin ribbon (250).
3 white embroidery stones (optional).
Small quantity of washable stuffing.
8 Vogue Star buttons (The Italian Collection, No. 813) — child's.
10 Vogue Star buttons (The Italian Collection, No. 816) — adult's.
1 pair No. 3¼mm (UK 10, US 3) needles, 1 pair No. 4mm (UK 10, US 3) needles — child's.
1 pair No. 5½mm (UK 5, US 8) needles, 1 pair No. 6½mm (UK 3, US 10) needles — adult's.
2 stitch holders.

7 THE FROGS

Sirdar Country Style Double Knitting x 50g balls (approx.)

SHADE	KEY	INCH 22 / CM 56	(24 / (61	26 / 66	28 / 71	30 / 76	32 / 81	34 / 86	36 / 91	38 / 96	40 / 102	42 / 107	44) / 112)
(477) Indian Yellow	A	2	(3	3	3	3	4	4	4	4	5	5	5)
(479) Emerald	B	1	(1	1	1	1	1	1	1	1	1	1	1)
(427) Banana	C						Small quantity						
(402) Cherry	D	3	(3	3	3	3	3	4	4	4	4	4	4)
(412) White	E	1	(1	1	1	1	1	1	1	1	1	1	1)
(417) Black (Embroidery)							Oddment						

1 pair No. 3¼mm (UK 10, US 3) needles, 1 pair No. 4mm (UK 8, US 5) needles.
2 stitch holders.

8 THE TEDDY BEARS

Sirdar Country Style Double Knitting x 50g balls (approx.)

SHADE	KEY	INCH 22 / CM 56	(24 / (61	26 / 66	28 / 71	30 / 76	32 / 81	34 / 86	36 / 91	38 / 96	40 / 102	42 / 107	44) / 112)
(412) White	A	3	(3	4	4	4	5	5	5	5	6	6)	
(417) Black	B						Small quantity						
(420) Lobelia	C						Small quantity						
(479) Emerald	D	1	(1	1	1	1	1	1	1	1	1	1	1)
(439) Dark Chocolate	E	1	(1	1	1	1	1	1	1	1	1	1	1)
(482) Majestic Mink	F	1	(1	1	1	1	1	1	1	1	1	1	1)
(495) Guard's Red	G	1	(1	1	1	1	1	1	1	1	1	1	1)
(449) Royal	H	1	(1	1	1	1	1	1	1	1	1	1	1)
(460) Corona Yellow	J						Small quantity						
(485) Turquoise	K	2	(2	3	3	3	4	4	4	4	5	5)	

2 pairs 15mm safety goo-goo eyes.
Small quantity of washable stuffing.
5in (12cm) 15mm red Offray Singleface Satin ribbon (250).
10in (25cm) 39mm Offray Ship Ahoy ribbon (Comb. 2 red).
1 pair No. 3¼mm (UK 10, US 3) needles, 1 pair No. 4mm (UK 8, US 5) needles.
2 stitch holders.

9 THE PENGUINS

Sirdar Wash 'n' Wear Double Crepe x 50g balls (approx.)

SHADE	KEY	INCH 22 / CM 56	(24 / (61	26 / 66	28 / 71	30 / 76	32 / 81	34 / 86	36 / 91	38 / 96	40 / 102	42 / 107	44) / 112)
(248) Peacock Blue	A	1	(1	1	1	1	1	2	2	2	2	2	2)
(238) Silver Blue	B	2	(2	2	3	3	3	4	4	4	5	5	5)
(275) Black	C	1	(1	1	1	1	1	1	1	1	1	1	1)
(251) White	D	1	(1	1	1	1	1	1	1	1	1	1	1)
(264) Hydrangea Blue	E	4	(4	4	4	5	5	6	6	6	7	7	7)
(284) Citron	F	1	(1	1	1	1	1	1	1	1	1	1	1)
(230) Imperial Purple	G	1	(1	1	1	1	1	1	1	1	1	1	1)
(287) Veridian	H	1	(1	1	1	1	1	1	1	1	1	1	1)
(278) Cherry	J	1	(1	1	1	1	1	1	1	1	1	1	1)

1 pair No. 3¼mm (UK 10, US 3) needles, 1 pair No. 4mm (UK 8, US 5) needles.
2 stitch holders.

10 NOAH'S ARK

Sirdar Country Style Double Knitting x 50g balls (approx.)

SHADE	KEY	INCH 22 / CM 56	(24 / (61	26 / 66	28 / 71	30 / 76	32 / 81	34 / 86	36 / 91	38 / 96	40 / 102	42 / 107	44) / 112)
(430) Magenta Flame	A	1	(1	1	1	1	1	1	1	1	1	1	1)
(420) Lobelia	B	1	(1	1	1	1	1	1	1	1	1	1	1)
(479) Emerald	C	1	(1	1	1	1	1	1	1	1	1	1	1)
(460) Corona Yellow	D	1	(1	1	1	1	1	1	1	1	1	1	1)
(495) Guard's Red	E	1	(1	1	1	1	1	1	1	1	1	1	1)
(444) Tropical Green	F	3	(4	4	4	5	5	5	5	5	6	6)	
(412) White	G	1	(1	1	1	1	1	1	1	1	1	1	1)
(417) Black	H						Small quantity						
(439) Dark Chocolate	J	1	(1	1	1	1	1	1	1	1	1	1	1)
(472) Stormcloud	K	2	(2	2	3	3	3	4	4	4	5	5)	
(477) Indian Yellow	L						Small quantity						
(482) Majestic Mink	M						Small quantity						
(419) Tartan Green	N						Small quantity						

2 20mm white pom-poms.
32in (81cm) 39mm Offray Ship Ahoy ribbon (Comb. 2 red).
1 pair No. 3¼mm (UK 10, US 3) needles, 1 pair No. 4mm (UK 8, US 5) needles.
2 stitch holders.

11   INSIDE THE ARK

Sirdar Country Style Double Knitting x 50g balls (approx.)

SHADE	KEY	INCH 24 CM 61	(26 (66	28 71	30 76	32 81	34 86	36 91	38 96	40 102	42 107	44) 112)
(495) Guard's Red	A	2	(2	2	2	2	3	3	3	3	3	3)
(479) Emerald	B	1	(2	2	2	2	3	3	3	3	3	3)
(417) Black	C	1	(1	1	1	1	1	1	1	1	1	1)
(460) Corona Yellow	D	1	(2	2	2	2	3	3	3	3	3	3)
(449) Royal	E	1	(1	1	2	2	3	3	3	3	3	3)
(404) Parchment	F	1	(1	1	1	1	1	1	1	1	1	1)
(453) Terracotta	G	1	(1	1	1	1	1	1	1	1	1	1)
(439) Dark Chocolate	H	1	(1	1	1	1	1	1	1	1	1	1)
(412) White	J	1	(1	1	1	1	1	1	1	1	1	1)
(434) Silver Cloud	K	1	(1	1	1	1	1	1	1	1	1	1)

4in (5cm) 7mm red Offray Singleface Satin ribbon (250).
1 pair No. 3¼mm (UK 10, US 3) needles, 1 pair No. 4mm (UK 8, US 5) needles.
2 stitch holders.

12   THE RAINBOW

Sirdar Silky Look Double Knitting x 50g balls (approx.) for the Child's
or alternatively Sirdar Country Style Double Knitting x 50 balls (approx.)
Sirdar Supreme Mohair x 50g balls (approx.) for the Adult's

SHADE	KEY	ONE SIZE Actual measurement: 35in (89cm)
Child's		
(981) Blue Frost	A	7
(429) Lupin (CS)*		6
(916) African Violet	B	1
(423) Imperial Purple (CS)*		1
(915) Pacific Blue	C	1
(461) Siren Jade (CS)*		1
(938) Tropical Green	D	1
(444) Tropical Green (CS)*		1
(938) Wild Honey	E	1
(460) Corona Yellow (CS)*		1
(914) Crimson	F	1
(402) Cherry (CS)*		1
(911) White	G	1
(412) White (CS)*		1

* (CS) = Sirdar Country Style D.K.
1 pair No. 3¼mm (UK 10, US 3) needles, 1 pair No. 4mm (UK 8, US 5) needles.
1 stitch holder and 2 safety pins.
8 rainbow buttons from Peapods to Zebras (address in Noah's Address Book
    on page 71).

Adult's		Actual measurement: 52in (132cm)
(975) Silky Blue	A	9
(945) Lavender	B	1
(991) Pacific Blue	C	1
(972) Tropical Green	D	1
(979) Wild Honey	E	1
(942) Carmine	F	1
(940) White	G	1

1 pair No. 4½mm (UK 7, US 6) needles, 1 pair No. 5½mm (UK 5, US 8) needles.
1 stitch holder and 2 safety pins.
10 rainbow buttons from Peapods to Zebras (address in Noah's Address Book
    on page 71).

Measurements

BASIC PATTERN A — MEASUREMENTS FOR PATTERNS No. 1, 3, 5, 7, 8, 10, 11													
To fit chest	IN	22	(24	26	28	30	32	34	36	38	40	42	44)
	CM	56	(61	66	71	76	81	86	91	96	102	107	112)
Actual measurement	IN	24½	(26½	29	31	33	35½	37½	40	42	44	46	48)
	CM	62	(67	74	78	84	90	95	102	107	112	117	122)
Length from back of neck	IN	17	(18	19¾	20¼	21½	24	28	28	28¼	28¼	28¼	28¼)
	CM	43	(46	50	51	55	61	71	71	72	72	72	72)
Sleeve length (adjustable)	IN	12	(14	15	16	17	18	18	19	19	19	20	20)
	CM	30	(35	38	41	43	46	46	48	48	48	51	51)

BASIC PATTERN A and B — MEASUREMENTS FOR PATTERN No. 4													
To fit chest	IN	22	(24	26	28	30	32	34	36	38	40	42	44)
	CM	56	(61	66	71	76	81	86	91	96	102	107	112)
Actual measurement	IN	26	(28	30	32	34	38	40	42	44	46	48	50)
	CM	66	(71	76	81	86	96	102	107	112	117	122	127)
Length from back of neck	IN	17	(18	19¾	20¼	21½	24	28	28	28¼	28¼	28¼	28¼)
	CM	43	(46	50	51	55	61	71	71	72	72	72	72)
Sleeve length (adjustable)	IN	12	(14	15	16	17	18	18	19	19	19	20	20)
	CM	30	(35	38	41	43	46	46	48	48	48	51	51)

BASIC PATTERN A and B — MEASUREMENTS FOR PATTERNS No. 2, 9													
To fit chest	IN	22	(24	26	28	30	32	34	36	38	40	42	44)
	CM	56	(61	66	71	76	81	86	91	96	102	107	112)
Actual measurement	IN	24½	(26½	28½	30½	32½	36	38	40	42	44	46	48)
	CM	62	(67	72	77	82	91	96	102	107	112	117	122)
Length from back of neck	IN	17	(18	19¾	20¼	22	24½	28	28½	28½	28½	28½	28½)
	CM	43	(46	50	51	56	62	71	72	73	73	73	73)
Sleeve length (adjustable)	IN	12	(14	15	16	17	18	18	19	19	19	20	20)
	CM	30	(35	38	41	43	46	46	48	48	48	51	51)

BASIC PATTERN A — MEASUREMENTS FOR PATTERN No. 6													
To fit chest	IN	22	(24	26	28	30	32	34	36	38	40	42	44)
	CM	56	(61	66	71	76	81	86	91	96	102	107	112)
Actual measurement	IN	24½	(26½	29	31	33	35½	38	40	42	44	46	48)
	CM	62	(67	74	78	84	90	96	102	107	112	117	122)
Length from back of neck	IN	17	(18	19¾	20¼	21½	24	29	29	29	29	29	29)
	CM	43	(46	50	51	55	61	74	74	74	74	74	74)
Sleeve length (adjustable)	IN	12	(14	15	16	17	18	19	19	19	19	20	20)
	CM	30	(35	38	41	43	46	48	48	48	48	51	51)

MEASUREMENTS FOR PATTERN No. 12		
	One size – Child's	One size – Adult's
To fit chest	24 – 32in 61 – 81cm	34 – 44in 86 – 112cm
Actual measurement	35in 89cm	52in 132cm
Length from back of neck	19in 48cm	29in 74cm
Sleeve length (adjustable)	17in 43cm	20in 51cm

There are two basic patterns to work from in this book, PATTERN A and PATTERN B, to enable you to knit the sweater or cardigan of your choice. Each pattern has been adapted for both children and adults and the instructions are given as clearly as possible to make the knitting of these garments as easy and as enjoyable as possible. Each pattern is star rated with either one, two or three stars. They are as follows:

* Suitable for a beginner
** Suitable for an average knitter
*** Suitable for an experienced knitter

A number of the designs have attachments added on afterwards, and clear instructions are given to complete each garment.

TENSION

The tension is given in PATTERN A and PATTERN B. This is the recommended tension for the yarn used and the measurements given using the exact tension, allowing 2 sts for the seams. It is very important to check your tension and use the correct needles. Remember that if you make the sweaters larger than the sizes recommended because

your tension is incorrect you may need more yarn. Similarly, if you make your sleeves longer you may need more yarn. The quantity of yarn recommended allows you to strand the background colour across the motifs, although block knitting, carrying the yarn up the work on the wrong side, is highly recommended to give a better finish (see Working with Colours on page 32).

ABBREVIATIONS

k = knit; p = purl; k1b = knit into back of stitch; k2tog = knit 2 sts together; p2tog = purl 2 sts together; st = stitch; sts = stitches; st st = stocking stitch (UK) or stockinette stitch (US); in = inches; cm = centimetres; cast off (UK) = Bind off (US); stocking stitch (stockinette stitch US) = 1 row knit, 1 row purl; twisted rib = knitting into the back of all the knit stitches; garter stitch = every row knit.

BASIC PATTERN A

TENSION

22 sts and 28 rows measure 4in (10cm) over st st on No. 4mm (UK 8, US 5) needles (or size needed to obtain this tension).

FRONT

With No. 3¼mm (UK 10, US 3) needles and appropriate colour for ribbing (as given in each individual pattern) cast on 65 (71, 77, 83, 89, 95, 101, 107, 113, 119, 125, 131) sts and work 12 (12, 14, 14, 16, 24, 24, 24, 24, 24, 24, 24) rows in Twisted Rib as follows:
ROW 1: k1, p1, *k1b, p1, repeat from * to last st, k1.
ROW 2: p1, k1b, *p1, k1b, repeat from * to last st, p1.
On the last row, increase 5 sts evenly along: 70 (76, 82, 88, 94, 100, 106, 112, 118, 124, 130, 136) sts. Change to No. 4mm (UK 8, US 5) needles and

work in st st as given in each individual pattern.
DIVIDE FOR THE NECK: k30 (33, 36, 38, 41, 44, 47, 50, 53, 56, 59, 62) sts, turn leaving remaining sts on a spare needle.
NEXT ROW: p2tog, purl to end of row.
NEXT ROW: knit to last 2 sts, k2tog. Continue decreasing at neck edge on every row until 26 (29, 31, 33, 35, 36, 39, 40, 43, 46, 49, 52) sts and then on alternate rows until 23 (25, 27, 30, 32, 32, 33, 35, 38, 39, 42, 45) sts. Work a further 12 (12, 13, 15, 15, 12, 12, 12, 12, 10, 10, 10) rows straight, finishing with right side facing.
NEXT ROW: Cast off 8 (8, 9, 10, 11, 11, 11, 12, 13, 13, 14, 15) sts, knit to end of row.
NEXT ROW: purl. Repeat the last two rows once more.
NEXT ROW: cast off remaining 7 (9, 9, 10, 10, 11, 11, 12, 13, 14, 15) sts. Put centre 10 (10, 10, 12, 12, 12, 12, 12, 12, 12, 12, 12) sts on a stitch holder and rejoin yarn to other side of neck. Work as for the first side, reversing all the shapings.

BACK

Work Twisted Rib as for Front in the same colour (as given in each individual pattern). Continue in st st following each pattern's instructions until the Back measures the same as the Front to the shoulder shapings:
NEXT 4 ROWS: Cast off 8 (8, 9, 10, 11, 11, 11, 12, 13, 13, 14, 15) sts work to end of row.
NEXT 2 ROWS: Cast off 7 (9, 9, 10, 10, 10, 11, 11, 12, 13, 14, 15) sts. Leave the remaining 24 (26, 28, 28, 30, 36, 40, 42, 42, 46, 46, 46) sts on a stitch holder.

SLEEVES

With No. 3¼mm (UK 10, US 3) needles and appropriate colour for ribbing (as given in each individual pattern), cast on 37 (39, 41, 43, 45, 47, 47, 49, 49, 49, 49, 49) sts and work 12 (12, 14, 14, 16, 20, 20, 20, 20, 20, 20, 20) rows in Twisted Rib as for Front. On the last row of Rib, increase 14

(14, 14, 14, 14, 14, 16, 16, 16, 18, 18, 20) evenly across: 51 (53, 55, 57, 59, 61, 63, 65, 65, 67, 67, 69) sts. Change to No. 4mm (UK 8, US 5) needles and work in st st increasing each end of the 5th and following 6th (6th, 6th, 6th, 6th, 4th, 4th, 4th, 4th, 4th, 4th, 4th) rows until 73 (75, 79, 83, 87, 101, 115, 119, 119, 121, 121, 121) sts. Continue until Sleeve measures 12 (14, 15, 16, 17, 18, 18, 19, 19, 19, 20, 20) in, 30 (36, 38, 41, 43, 46, 46, 48, 48, 48, 51, 51) cm or the length required. Cast off loosely.

NECKBAND

With right sides together sew left shoulder seam with a fine back stitch. Using the appropriate colour and No. 3¼mm (UK 10, US 3) needles, k24 (26, 28, 28, 30, 36, 40, 42, 42, 46, 46, 46) sts across Back, pick up and k28 (28, 30, 32, 32, 34, 34, 36, 38, 38, 38, 38) sts down side of neck, k10 (10, 10, 12, 12, 12, 12, 12, 12, 12, 12, 12) sts from stitch holder, pick up and k28 (28, 30, 32, 32, 34, 34, 36, 38, 38, 38, 38) sts up other side of neck: 90 (92, 98, 104, 106, 116, 120, 126, 130, 134, 134, 134) sts. Work 6 (6, 8, 8, 8, 8, 8, 8, 8, 8, 8, 8) rows of Twisted Rib, knit 1 row (hem line), then work a further 6 (6, 8, 8, 8, 8, 8, 8, 8, 8, 8, 8) rows of Twisted Rib. Cast off loosely with a No. 4mm (UK 8, US 5) needle.
Darn in all the loose ends from the motifs.

FINISHING

Press each piece carefully under a dry cloth or according to the instructions on the ball band. Work any embroidery required and sew on attachments as indicated in each individual instruction. Sew the other shoulder seam together with a fine back stitch. Fold the neckband in half to the wrong side and sew loosely in place. With a fine back stitch, sew in sleeves, sew up side and sleeve seams, oversewing the ribbing. Press again, if necessary, avoiding any attachments fixed or sewn on. Follow the washing instructions on the ball band. When safety eyes have been used, do not tumble dry.

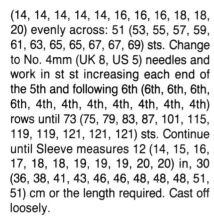

BASIC PATTERN B

TENSION

24 sts and 30 rows measure 4in (10cm) over st st on No. 4mm (UK 8, US 5) needles (or size needed to obtain this tension).

FRONT

With No. 3¼mm (UK 10, US 3) needles and appropriate colour for ribbing (as given in each individual pattern), cast on 70 (76, 82, 88, 94, 104, 110, 116, 122, 128, 134, 140) sts and work 12 (12, 14, 14, 16, 24, 24, 24, 24, 24, 24, 24) rows in Twisted Rib as follows: k1, p1, *k1b, p1, repeat from * to end of row. On the last row, increase 6 sts evenly along: 76 (82, 88, 94, 100, 110, 116, 122, 128, 134, 140, 146) sts. Change to No. 4mm (UK 8, US 5) needles and work in st st as given in each individual pattern.
DIVIDE FOR THE NECK: k33 (36, 39, 41, 44, 49, 52, 55, 58, 61, 64, 67) sts, turn leaving remaining sts on a spare needle.
**NEXT ROW: p2tog, purl to end of row.
NEXT ROW: knit to last 2 sts, k2tog. Continue decreasing at neck edge until 27 (30, 33, 35, 38, 39, 42, 45, 48, 51, 54, 57) sts and then on alternate rows until 24 (27, 29, 30, 33, 34, 36, 39, 42, 44, 47, 50) sts. Work a further 10 (10, 12, 10, 12, 10, 12, 10, 12, 10, 10, 10) rows straight, finishing with right side facing.
NEXT ROW: cast off 8 (9, 10, 10, 11, 11, 12, 13, 14, 15, 16, 17) sts, knit to end of row.
NEXT ROW: purl. Repeat the last

two rows once more.
NEXT ROW: cast off the remaining 8 (9, 9, 10, 11, 12, 12, 13, 14, 14, 15, 16) sts.** Put centre 10 (10, 10, 12, 12, 12, 12, 12, 12, 12, 12, 12) sts on a stitch holder and rejoin yarn to other side of neck. Work as for first side reversing all the shapings.

BACK

Work Rib as for Front in the same colour (as given in each individual pattern). Continue in st st following each pattern's instructions until the Back measures the same as the Front to the shoulder shapings:
NEXT 4 ROWS: Cast off 8 (9, 10, 10, 11, 11, 12, 13, 14, 15, 16, 17) sts, work to end of row.
NEXT 2 ROWS: Cast off 8 (9, 9, 10, 11, 12, 12, 13, 14, 14, 15, 16). Leave the remaining 28 (28, 30, 34, 34, 42, 44, 44, 44, 46, 46, 46) sts on a stitch holder.

SLEEVES

Follow PATTERN A.

NECKBAND

With right sides together sew left shoulder seam with a fine back stitch. Using the appropriate colour and No. 3¼mm (UK 10, US 3) needles, k28 (28, 30, 34, 34, 42, 44, 44, 44, 46, 46, 46) sts across Back, pick up and k28 (28, 30, 32, 32, 34, 34, 36, 38, 38, 38, 38) sts down side of neck, k10 (10, 10, 12, 12, 12, 12, 12, 12, 12, 12, 12) sts from stitch holder, pick up and k28 (28, 30, 32, 32, 34, 34, 36, 38, 38, 38, 38) sts up on other side of neck: 94 (94, 100, 110, 110, 122, 124, 128, 132, 134, 134, 134) sts. Work 6 (6, 8, 8, 8, 8, 8, 8, 8, 8, 8, 8) rows in Twisted Rib, knit 1 row (hem line), then work a further 6 (6, 8, 8, 8, 8, 8, 8, 8, 8, 8, 8) rows of Twisted Rib.
Cast off loosely with a No. 4mm (UK 8, US 5) needle.
Darn in all the loose ends from the motifs.

FINISHING

Follow PATTERN A.

1 THE LIONS***

MEASUREMENTS
To fit Chest 22-44in (56-112cm)
See page 37

MATERIALS
See page 34

WORKING NOTES
See page 32

ABBREVIATIONS
See page 38

BASIC INSTRUCTIONS
Pattern A on page 38

FRONT

Using Tartan Green (A), cast on the required number of sts as in PATTERN A and work Rib. Change to No. 4mm (UK 8, US 5) needles and work in st st beginning with a knit row for 2 (6, 16, 16, 22, 28, 56, 54, 54, 54, 54, 54) rows. Now work from Chart 1, changing colours where necessary, as follows:

The first two rows are in Tartan Green (A).
ROW 3: Beginning and ending row with Pastel Jade (B), k0 (3, 6, 9, 12, 15, 18, 21, 24, 27, 30, 33) sts, work 3rd row of chart, k0 (3, 6, 9, 12, 15, 18, 21, 24, 27, 30, 33) sts.

ROW 4: p0 (3, 6, 9, 12, 15, 18, 21, 24, 27, 30, 33) sts, work 4th row of chart, p0 (3, 6, 9, 12, 15, 18, 21, 24, 27, 30, 33) sts.
Continue working from Chart 1 until Row 17. At the same time as following Chart 1, work the paw prints by following Chart 3 continuing the paw prints to the end of the row, according to size. Continue working from Chart 1 until Row 37. Follow Chart 5 (a), for left hand side of work and Chart 5 (b), for right hand side to work the hedge either side of Chart 1. Continue until Chart 1 is complete. Work a further 1 (5, 5, 9, 9, 13, 13, 15, 15, 17, 17, 17) rows. DIVIDE FOR THE NECK: Follow PATTERN A.

BACK

Work as for Front until Row 16 of Chart 1 has been completed. Then follow Chart 2 for the Lioness and AT THE SAME TIME work the paw prints in by following Chart 4 according to size. Continue working from Chart 2 until Row 21.

Charts 5 (a) and (b) show the hedge to be knitted either side of the Chart. When Chart 2 is completed continue working Back in Lupin (E) until Back measures the same as the Front. Complete as in PATTERN A.

RIGHT SLEEVE

Using Tartan Green (A) follow PATTERN A

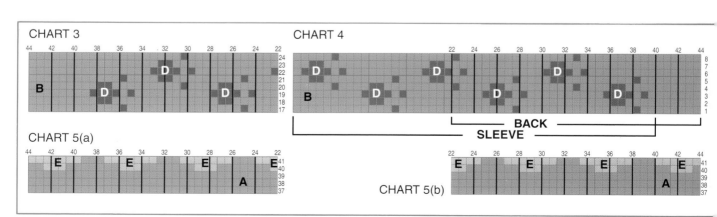

CHART 3

CHART 4

CHART 5(a)

CHART 5(b)

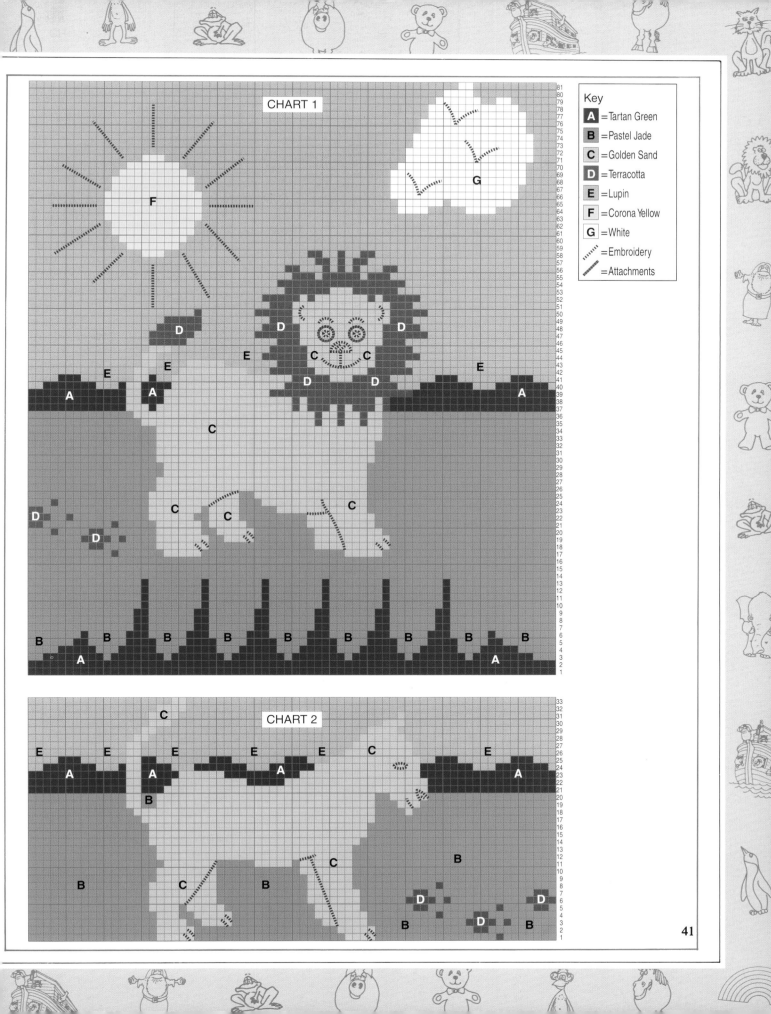

CHART 1

CHART 2

Key

A = Tartan Green
B = Pastel Jade
C = Golden Sand
D = Terracotta
E = Lupin
F = Corona Yellow
G = White

= Embroidery

= Attachments

41

for Rib. Change to No. 4mm (UK 8, US 5) needles and Pastel Jade (B), work in st st as in PATTERN A. AT THE SAME TIME when 16 (16, 30, 30, 40, 40, 40, 44, 44, 44, 44, 44) rows have been worked follow Chart 4 — the six paw prints marked from 0 to 40, placing them in the centre of the Sleeve. Work another 8 rows. Break off Pastel Jade (B), join in Tartan Green (A) and work the hedge following Chart 5 (b) repeating the pattern.

Continue working in Lupin (E) until Sleeve measures the required length as in PAT-TERN A.

LEFT SLEEVE

Work as for Right Sleeve omitting the paw prints.

NECKBAND

Using Lupin (E) follow PATTERN A.

BACK OF HEAD

Using No. 4mm (UK 8, US 5) needles and Golden Sand (C) cast on 13 sts and work 12 rows in st st. Cast off loosely.

Darn in all the loose ends from the motifs.

EMBROIDERY
(as indicated on Charts 1 and 2)

Attach 2 — 9mm safety eyes to Lion's face as indicated in Working Notes, or embroider eyes, as shown in the section on Embroidery. Using Black yarn, work the nose in satin stitch and the mouth, ears and birds in back stitch. Using Terracotta (D), embroider the legs and paws. Using Corona Yellow (F), embroider the sun's rays in back stitch. With wrong sides together sew the back of the head to the back of the Lion's face to encase the back of the eyes. Add a little stuffing to make the face stand out.

FINISHING

Follow PATTERN A.

| 2 | # THE ELEPHANTS** |

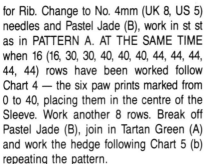

MEASUREMENTS
To fit Chest 22-44in (56-112cm)
See page 37

MATERIALS
See page 34

WORKING NOTES
See page 32

ABBREVIATIONS
See page 38

BASIC INSTRUCTIONS

PATTERN A on page 38 and PATTERN B on page 39

TENSION
PATTERN B

RIGHT FRONT

Using Citron (A) and No. 3¼mm (UK 10, US 3) needles, cast on 41 (44, 47, 50, 53, 58, 61, 64, 67, 70, 73, 76) sts and work 2 rows in Twisted Rib.

NEXT ROW (buttonhole row): rib 2, cast off 2 sts, rib to end of row.

NEXT ROW: rib to last 4 sts, cast on 2 sts (over cast off sts), rib 2 sts. Work Rib for another 8 (8, 10, 10, 12, 20, 20, 20, 20, 20, 20, 20) rows.

On the last row increase 3 sts evenly along the first 35 (38, 41, 44, 47, 52, 55, 58, 61, 64, 67, 70) sts. Leave the last 6 sts on a safety pin: 38 (41, 44, 47, 50, 55, 58, 61, 64, 67, 70, 73) sts. Change to No. 4mm (UK 8, US 5) needles and work in st st for 10 (10, 12, 12, 14, 14, 20, 20, 20, 20, 20, 20) rows. Work Chart 3 repeating the 11 sts across the row. When Chart 3 is complete, using Citron (A) work a further 24 (26, 38, 38, 44, 56, 70, 70, 72, 72, 72, 72) rows. Work Chart 1 as follows, joining in colours where necessary:

ROW 1: k6 (for all sizes), work 1st row of chart, k7 (10, 13, 16, 19, 24, 27, 30, 33, 36, 39, 42) sts.

ROW 2: p7 (10, 13, 16, 19, 24, 27, 30, 33, 36, 39, 42) sts, work 2nd row of chart, p6 (for all sizes).

Continue working from chart until Row 42 is complete. Work a further 4 (8, 8, 12, 12, 16, 16, 18, 18, 20, 20, 20) rows.

NECK DECREASING: Cast of 5 (5, 5, 6, 6, 6, 6, 6, 6, 6, 6, 6) sts, knit to end of row. Follow PATTERN B from ** to ** *reversing the shapings.*

LEFT FRONT

Using Citron (A) work as for Right Front omitting the buttonhole and on the last row of Rib, increase 3 sts evenly across, placing the first 6 sts on a safety pin. Change to No. 4mm (UK 8, US 5) needles and work in st st for 10 (10, 12, 12, 14, 14, 20, 20, 20, 20, 20, 20) rows. Work Chart 2 as follows, joining in colours where necessary:

ROW 1: k6 (9, 12, 15, 18, 23, 26, 29, 32, 35, 38, 41) sts, work 1st row of chart, k6 (for all sizes).

ROW 2: p6 (for all sizes), work 2nd row of chart, p6 (9, 12, 15, 18, 23, 26, 29, 32, 35, 38, 41) sts. Continue working from chart until Row 42 is completed.

Work a further 23 (25, 37, 37, 43, 55, 69, 69, 71, 71, 71, 71) rows. With wrong side facing, on a purl row, work Chart 3 (working from right to left), repeating the 11 sts across the row. When chart is complete, work a further 4 (8, 8, 12, 12, 16, 16, 18, 18, 20, 20, 20) rows.

NECK DECREASING: With wrong side facing, cast off 5 (5, 5, 6, 6, 6, 6, 6, 6, 6, 6, 6) sts, purl to end of row. Knit 1 row. Follow PATTERN B from ** to **.

BACK

Using Citron (A) and No. 3¼mm (UK 10, US 3) needles cast on the required number of sts given in PATTERN B for the FRONT and work Rib accordingly. Change to No. 4mm (UK 8, US 5) needles and work 10 (10, 12, 12, 14, 14, 20, 20, 20, 20, 20, 20) rows in st st. Work Chart 3 repeating the 11 sts across the row. When chart is complete, using Citron (A) work a further 56 (58, 70, 70, 76, 88, 102, 102, 104, 104, 104, 104) rows. Repeat Chart 3 again repeating the 11 sts across the row. When Chart 3 is complete, using Citron (A) continue until Back measures the same as the Front to the shoulder shapings. Work shoulder shapings as in PATTERN B.

SLEEVES (Both the same)

Using Citron (A) follow PATTERN A. AT THE SAME TIME after 8 rows (for all sizes) have been worked in st st, follow Chart 3 repeating the 11 sts across the row. When Chart 3 is complete, continue in Citron (A) as in PATTERN A.

LEFT BAND

Transfer the sts from the safety pin on to a No. 3¼mm (UK 10, US 3) needle and work in Twisted Rib until the Band reaches the neck when slightly stretched. Leave sts on a safety pin and sew band to Left Front by oversewing.

RIGHT BAND (Buttonhole Band)

Place 8 (8, 8, 8, 8, 10, 10, 10, 10, 10, 10, 10) sewing pins equally spaced down Left Band, including one opposite the buttonhole in the Rib, and allowing one, 3 rows after the neckband has been started. Work as for Left Band working the buttonholes in the appropriate places, as before in the Rib. When Band is complete with 7 (7, 7, 7, 7, 9, 9, 9, 9, 9, 9, 9) buttonholes and measures the same at the Left Band, sew in place.

NECKBAND

Sew together both shoulder seams with a fine back stitch. Using Citron (A) and No. 3¼mm (UK 10, US 3) needles, rib across 6 sts from Band, pick up and k28 (28, 30, 32, 32, 34, 34, 36, 38, 38, 38, 38) sts up side of neck, k28 (28, 30, 34, 34, 42, 44, 44, 46, 46, 46) sts across Back, pick up and k28 (28, 30, 32, 32, 34, 34, 36, 38, 38, 38, 38) sts down side of neck, rib 6 from safety pin: 96 (96, 102, 110, 110, 122, 124, 128, 132, 134, 134, 134) sts. Rib 3 rows in Twisted Rib. NEXT ROW: rib 2, cast off 2 sts, rib to end of row. NEXT

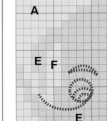

CHART 1

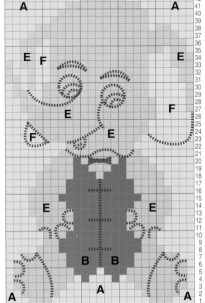

CHART 2

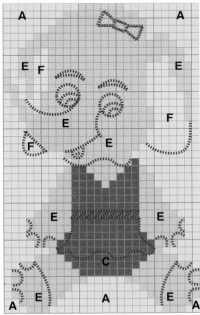

CHART 3

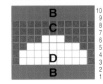

Key

A	= Citron (Yellow)
B	= Electric Blue
C	= Cherry
D	= White
E	= Silver Blue
F	= Romantic Pink
⁄⁄⁄	= Embroidery
⁄⁄	= Attachments

ROW: Rib to last 4 sts, cast on 2 sts, rib 2. Work 4 more rows in rib for all sizes. Cast off loosely.
Darn in all the loose ends from the motifs.

EMBROIDERY
(as indicated on Charts 1 and 2)

Using White (D), embroider the divides on the elephant's trunks, faces, chins, feet and waistcoat in a back stitch. Embroider the eyes as in the diagram in the section on Embroidery, in White (D), Electric Blue (B) and Black. Using White (D), embroider the circles on the elephants' feet. Using Black, embroider the eyebrows. Using Silver Blue (E) outline the elephants' ears between the Romantic Pink (F) and the Citron (A) with a back stitch. Using Cherry (C) embroider 6 french knots on the waistcoat. Using the 15mm Red ribbon, make two bows and sew one on the male elephant as a bow tie and the other on the female elephant's head. Gather a length of the 23mm Electric Blue ribbon and sew down to the female elephant's waist, then sew a straight piece of the 7mm White ribbon across the top for a belt. Sew on the appropriate number of buttons.

FINISHING

Follow PATTERN A.

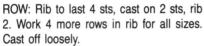

3 THE MONKEYS**

MEASUREMENTS
To fit Chest 22-44in (56-112cm)
See page 37

MATERIALS
See page 34

WORKING NOTES
See page 32

ABBREVIATIONS
See page 38

BASIC INSTRUCTIONS
PATTERN A on page 38

FRONT

Using Cream (A), cast on the required number of stitches as in PATTERN A and work Rib. Change to No. 4mm (UK 8, US 5) needles and beginning with a knit row, work as follows:
1st ROW: k65 (68, 71, 74, 77, 80, 83, 86, 89, 92, 95, 98) sts in Cream (A), join in Majestic Mink (B) and k5 (8, 11, 14, 17, 20, 23, 26, 29, 32, 35, 38) sts for the tree trunk.
2nd ROW: p5 (8, 11, 14, 17, 20, 23, 26, 29, 32, 35, 38) sts in Majestic Mink (B), twist the colours over one another once to avoid a hole, complete the row using Cream (A). Work a further 10 (14, 24, 24, 30, 36, 64, 62, 62, 62, 62, 62) rows. Now work from Chart 1, changing colours where necessary, as follows:
ROW 1: k0 (3, 6, 9, 12, 15, 18, 21, 24, 27, 30, 33) sts, work 1st row of chart, k0 (3, 6, 9, 12, 15, 18, 21, 24, 27, 30, 33) sts.
ROW 2: p0 (3, 6, 9, 12, 15, 18, 21, 24, 27, 30, 33) sts, work 2nd row of chart, p0 (3, 6, 9, 12, 15, 18, 21, 24, 27, 30, 33) sts.
NOTE: When working row 12, complete the row in Majestic Mink (B). Continue working the branch until row 18 is complete. Break off Majestic Mink (B) and join in Cream. Continue until chart is completed. Work a further 3 (7, 7, 11, 11, 15, 15, 17, 17, 19, 19, 19) rows.
DIVIDE FOR THE NECK: Follow PATTERN A.

BACK

Work Rib as for Front. Change to No. 4mm (UK 8, US 5) needles and work in st st beginning with a purl row as follows:
1st ROW: p65 (68, 71, 74, 77, 80, 83, 86, 89, 92, 95, 98) sts in Cream (A), join in Majestic Mink (B) and p5 (8, 11, 14, 17, 20, 23, 26, 29, 32, 35, 38) sts for the tree trunk. Continue working the two colours, twisting as before.
Work a further 11 (15, 25, 25, 31, 37, 65, 63, 63, 63, 63, 63) rows. Work from chart, the 1st row being a purl row working from

right to left on the chart, as follows:
ROW 1: p0 (3, 6, 9, 12, 15, 18, 21, 24, 27, 30, 33) sts, work 1st row of chart, p0 (3, 6, 9, 12, 15, 18, 21, 24, 27, 30, 33) sts.
ROW 2: k0 (3, 6, 9, 12, 15, 18, 21, 24, 27, 30, 33) sts, work 2nd row of chart, k0 (3, 6, 9, 12, 15, 18, 21, 24, 27, 30, 33) sts.
When chart is complete continue working the tree trunk (Majestic Mink (B)) and Cream (A) until the Back measures the same as the Front. Complete as in PATTERN A.

SLEEVES (Both the same)

Using Cream (A) follow PATTERN A for Rib. Change to No. 4mm (UK 8, US 5) needles and work as follows:
1st ROW: k18 (19, 20, 21, 22, 23, 24, 25, 25, 26, 26, 27) sts in Cream (A), join in Emerald (C), k5, join in Indian Yellow (E) k5, join in a separate ball of Emerald (C) k5, join in separate ball of Cream (A) and k18 (19, 20, 21, 22, 23, 24, 25, 25, 26, 26, 27) sts.
Continue the stripes up the centre of the Sleeve, twisting each colour over the next on each row. Complete Sleeve as in PATTERN A.

NECKBAND

Using Cream (A) follow PATTERN A. Darn in all loose ends from the motifs.

EMBROIDERY
(as indicated on chart)

For Front and Back, using Black (D), embroider the nose in satin stitch, work the divide on the face, mouth and eyebrows in back stitch. Embroider the eyes as in the diagram in the section on Embroidery using White and Black (D). Embroider two dots on the nose with White. With an oddment of Red embroider the tongue. With Majestic Mink (B) outline the banana and with Golden Sand (F) embroider the arm, leg and toes on the monkeys. Using Cream (A) embroider the leaves with a back stitch.

FINISHING

Follow PATTERN A.

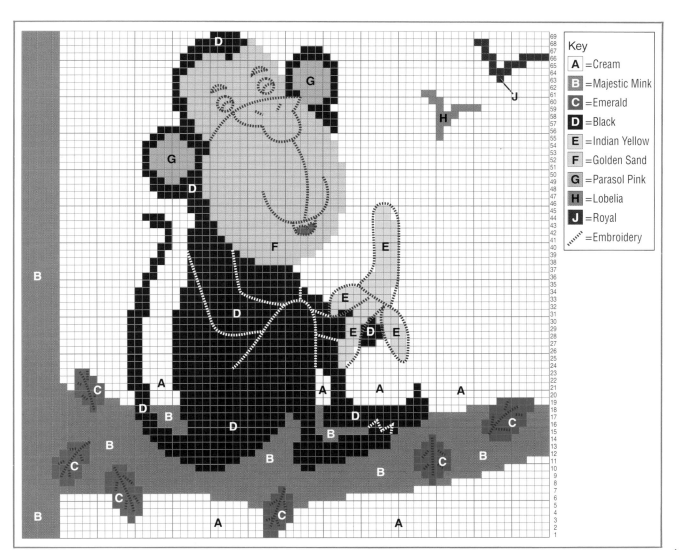

Key

A	=Cream
B	=Majestic Mink
C	=Emerald
D	=Black
E	=Indian Yellow
F	=Golden Sand
G	=Parasol Pink
H	=Lobelia
J	=Royal
⋯⋯⋯	=Embroidery

THE PIGS**

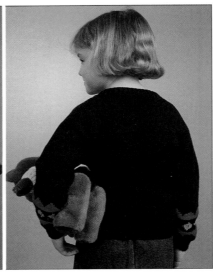

MEASUREMENTS
To fit Chest 22-44in (56-112cm)
See page 37

MATERIALS
See page 34

WORKING NOTES
See page 32

ABBREVIATIONS
See page 38

BASIC INSTRUCTIONS
*PATTERN A on page 38
and PATTERN B on page 39*

TENSION
PATTERN A

RIGHT FRONT

Using Navy (A) and No. 3¼mm (UK 10, US 3) needles, cast on 41 (44, 47, 50, 53, 58, 61, 64, 67, 70, 73, 76) sts and work 2 rows in Twisted Rib.
NEXT ROW (buttonhole row): rib 2, cast off 2 sts, rib to end of row.
NEXT ROW: rib to last 4 sts, cast on 2 sts (over cast off sts), rib 2 sts. Work Rib for another 8 (8, 10, 10, 12, 20, 20, 20, 20, 20, 20) rows.
On the last row increase 3 sts evenly along the first 35 (38, 41, 44, 47, 52, 55, 58, 61, 64, 67, 70) sts. Leave the last 6 sts on a safety pin: 38 (41, 44, 47, 50, 55, 58, 61, 64, 67, 70, 73) sts. Change to No. 4mm (UK 8, US 5) needles and work in st

st for 8 (10, 12, 12, 14, 20, 30, 30, 32, 32, 32, 32) rows. Work Chart 1 as follows, joining in colours where necessary:
ROW 1: k3 (6, 6, 6, 6, 6, 6, 6, 6, 6, 6, 6) sts, work 1st row of chart, k6 (6, 9, 12, 15, 20, 23, 26, 29, 32, 35, 38) sts.
ROW 2: p6 (6, 9, 12, 15, 20, 23, 26, 29, 32, 35, 38) sts, work 2nd row of chart, p3 (6, 6, 6, 6, 6, 6, 6, 6, 6, 6, 6) sts.
Continue working from chart until Row 67 is complete. Work a further 15 (19, 31, 35, 41, 51, 61, 63, 63, 65, 65, 65) rows.
NECK DECREASING: Cast off 5 (5, 5, 6, 6, 6, 6, 6, 6, 6, 6, 6) sts, knit to end of row. Follow PATTERN B ** to ** reversing the shapings.

LEFT FRONT

Work as for Right Front omitting the buttonhole increasing on the last row of Rib leaving the first 6 sts on a safety pin. Continue as Right Front to where the chart begins. Work Chart 2 as follows, joining in the colours where necessary:
ROW 1: k6 (6, 9, 12, 15, 20, 23, 26, 29, 32, 35, 38) sts, work 1st row of chart, k3 (6, 6, 6, 6, 6, 6, 6, 6, 6, 6, 6) sts.
ROW 2: p3 (6, 6, 6, 6, 6, 6, 6, 6, 6, 6, 6) sts, work 2nd row of chart, p6 (6, 9, 12, 15, 20, 23, 26, 29, 32, 35, 38) sts.
Continue working from chart until Row 74 is complete. Work a further 7 (11, 23, 27, 33, 43, 53, 55, 55, 57, 57, 57) rows.

NECK DECREASING: With wrong side facing, cast off 5 (5, 5, 6, 6, 6, 6, 6, 6, 6, 6, 6) sts, purl to end of row. Knit 1 row. Follow PATTERN B from ** to **.

BACK

Using Navy (A) follow PATTERN B.

SLEEVES (Both the same)

Using Navy (A) follow PATTERN A. When 6 rows of st st have been worked (for all sizes) follow Chart 3 according to size. Complete Sleeve as in PATTERN A.

LEFT AND RIGHT BANDS

Follow pattern for Elephants.

NECKBAND

Using Navy (A) follow pattern for Elephants.
Darn in all the loose ends from the motifs.

EMBROIDERY
(as indicated on Charts 1 and 2)

Using an oddment of Grey yarn, embroider the Pigs' eyes as in the diagram in the section on Embroidery. Using Grey embroider the pigs' ears, eyebrows, noses, mouths, divides for arms, etc., in back stitch. Using Parisian Pink (D) embroider two lines vertically on the bow on the girl pig's head. Using the 39mm Giant Dots ribbon, sew two strips together — one overlapping the other by ½in (1.5cm). Gather the top and folding under the ends, sew securely to the girl pig's waist. Sew the 9mm Blue Mist ribbon across the top of the skirt for the belt and sew 2 pearls on top. On the boy pig, sew the 9mm Blue Mist ribbon on for braces and then sew the 12mm Confetti Dot ribbon on for the belt and sew two pearls on. Make a bow from the 23mm wide Confetti Dot ribbon and sew securely under his chin. Sew the 7mm Electric Blue Singleface Satin ribbon across his hat. Sew the appropriate number of buttons on opposite the buttonholes.

FINISHING

Follow PATTERN A.

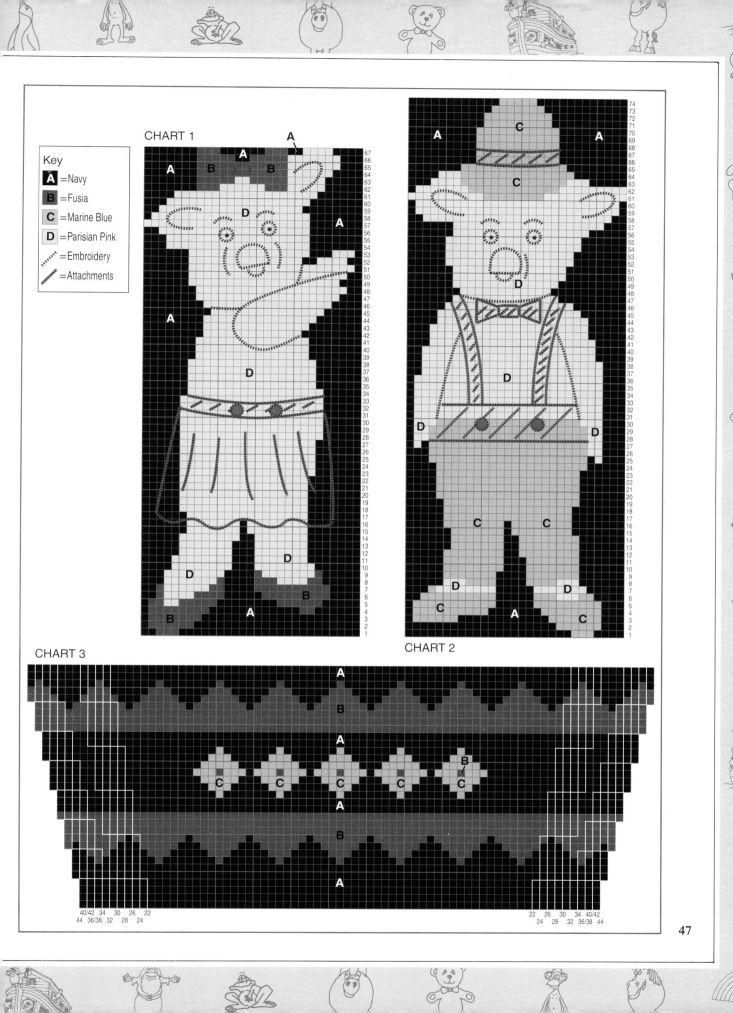

MEASUREMENTS
To fit Chest 24-44in (61-112cm)
See page 37

MATERIALS
See page 34

WORKING NOTES
See page 32

ABBREVIATIONS
See page 38

BASIC INSTRUCTIONS
PATTERN A on page 38

FRONT

(NOTE: The first size is a 24in (61cm) before the brackets.)
Using Emerald (A), cast on the required number of sts as in PATTERN A and work Rib. Change to No. 4mm (UK 8, US 5) needles and work in st st beginning with a knit row for 2 (4, 4, 4, 10, 16, 14, 14, 14, 14, 14) rows. Join in Parchment (B) and work Chart 1, all sizes starting from right hand side and repeating the pattern across the work. When Chart 1 is complete, work a further 2 (10, 10, 16, 16, 38, 38, 38, 38, 38, 38) rows in Emerald (A). Work Chart 2, joining colours in

where necessary, as follows:
ROW 1: k0 (3, 6, 9, 12, 15, 18, 21, 24, 27, 30) sts, work 1st row of chart, k0 (3, 6, 9, 12, 15, 18, 21, 24, 27, 30) sts.
ROW 2: p0 (3, 6, 9, 12, 15, 18, 21, 24, 27, 30) sts, work 2nd row of chart, p0 (3, 6, 9, 12, 15, 18, 21, 24, 27, 30) sts. Continue working from chart.
NOTE: At the beginning of Row 36, break off Indian Yellow (E) and join in Saxe (H). When chart is complete work a further 5 (5, 9, 9, 13, 13, 15, 15, 17, 17, 17) rows.
DIVIDE FOR THE NECK: Follow PATTERN A.

BACK

Work as for Front. When Chart 2 is completed continue working in st st until the Back measures the same as the Front to the shoulder shapings. Complete as in PATTERN A.

SLEEVES (Both the same)

Remember this pattern starts with a 24in (61cm). Using Emerald (A) follow PATTERN A for the Rib. Change to No. 4mm (UK 8, US 5) needles and follow PATTERN A. AT THE SAME TIME work

4 (4, 4, 4, 8, 8, 8, 8, 8, 8, 8) rows in st st from Rib. Join in Parchment (B) and work Chart 1, all sizes starting from the right hand side of chart. When chart is completed work a further 28 (28, 28, 28, 30, 30, 30, 30, 30, 30, 30) rows. Break off Emerald (A) and using Saxe (H) follow Chart 3, placing the 47 sts central in the Sleeve. When Chart 3 is complete finish Sleeve as in PATTERN A.

NECKBAND

Using Saxe (H) follow PATTERN A. Remember this pattern starts from a 24in (61cm).
Darn in all loose ends from the motifs.

EMBROIDERY
(as indicated on chart)

For Front and Back, using an oddment of Dark Grey, embroider the lines dividing the horses' legs and the features on their heads in back stitch. Using Black (C), embroider three birds on the cloud. Using the Mohair, attach the mane by looping the yarn along the mane line and then fixing in place by back stitching over it, as in the diagram in the section on Embroidery, then cut to the required length. For the tail, cut 4 – 9in (23cm) lengths of Mohair, fold in half and secure to the horse, as in the diagram in the section on Embroidery. Cut to the required length.

FINISHING

Follow PATTERN A.

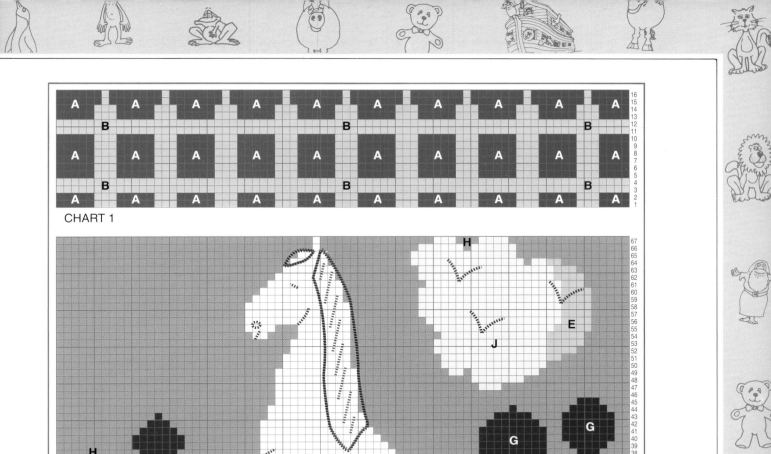

CHART 1

CHART 2

CHART 3

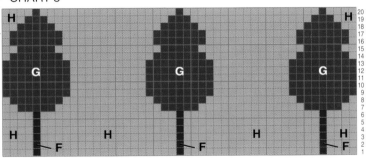

Key

A	=Emerald	**G**	=Tartan Green
B	=Parchment	**H**	=Saxe
C	=Black	**J**	=Stormcloud
D	=White		=Embroidery
E	=Indian Yellow		=Attachments
F	=Dark Chocolate		

49

MEASUREMENTS
To fit Chest 22-44in (56-112cm)
See page 37

MATERIALS
See page 35

WORKING NOTES
See page 32

ABBREVIATIONS
See page 38

BASIC INSTRUCTIONS
PATTERN A on page 38

NOTE: The instructions for this cardigan are given in Double Knitting yarn for sizes 22-32in (56-81cm) and in Chunky for sizes 34-44in (86-112cm).

TENSION: 22-32in (56-81cm): as PATTERN A. 34-44in (86-112cm): 14 sts and 19 rows measure 4in (10cm) over st st on No. 6½mm (UK 3, US 10) needles (or size needed to obtain this tension).

BACK

Using Pastel Jade (A) and No. 3¼mm (UK 10, US 3) needles for the Child's and No. 5½mm (UK 5, US 8) needles for the Adult's, cast on 65 (71, 77, 83, 89, 95, 65, 69, 73, 77, 81, 85) sts and work 12 (12, 14, 14, 16, 24, 14, 14, 14, 14, 14, 14) rows in Twisted Rib as PATTERN A. On the last row increase 5 sts evenly along for all sizes: 70 (76, 82, 88, 94, 100, 70, 74, 78, 82, 86, 90) sts. Change to No. 4mm (UK 8, US 5) needles for the Child's and No. 6½mm (UK 3, US 10) needles for the Adult's and work in st st for 22 (26, 36, 36, 42, 48, 64, 64, 64, 64, 64, 64) rows. Break off Pastel Jade (A) and work Fence as follows:

1st ROW: *k3 in Cardinal (B), k1 in Parchment (C), repeat from * to last 2 (0, 2, 0, 2, 0, 2, 2, 2, 2, 2, 2) sts, work last sts in Cardinal (B).

2nd ROW: Purl the Cardinal (B) sts with Cardinal (B) and the Parchment (C) sts with Parchment (C). Work a further 22 (22, 22, 22, 22, 22, 20, 20, 20, 20, 20, 20) rows in the same manner. Break off Cardinal (B) and Parchment (C) and join in Saxe (D) and work 60 (66, 68, 72, 74, 78, 44, 44, 44, 44, 44, 44) rows. Shape shoulders as follows:

NEXT 4 ROWS: Cast off 8 (8, 9, 10, 11, 11, 7, 8, 8, 9, 9, 10) sts, work to end of row.
NEXT 2 ROWS: Cast off 7 (9, 9, 10, 10, 10, 7, 7, 8, 8, 9, 9) sts, work to end of row. Leave the remaining 24 (26, 28, 28, 30, 36, 28, 28, 30, 30, 32, 32) sts on a stitch holder.

LEFT FRONT

Using Pastel Jade (A) and No. 3¼mm (UK 10, US 3) needles for the Child's and No. 5½mm (UK 5, US 8) needles for the Adult's, cast on 39 (42, 45, 48, 51, 54, 39, 41, 43, 45, 47, 49) sts and work in Twisted Rib as for Back. On the last row rib 6 sts and leave them on a safety pin for the Band, then increase 2 sts evenly along for all sizes: 35 (38, 41, 44, 47, 50, 35, 37, 39, 41, 43, 45) sts. Change to No. 4mm (UK 8, US 5) needles for the Child's and No. 6½mm (UK 3, US 10) needles for the Adult's and work in st st for 22 (26, 36, 36, 42, 48, 64, 64, 64, 64, 64, 64) rows. Break off Pastel Jade (A) and work Fence as follows:

NEXT ROW: K3 (2, 1, 0, 3, 2, 3, 1, 3, 1, 3, 1) sts in Cardinal (B), k1 in Parchment (C), *k3 in Cardinal (B), k1 in Parchment (C), repeat from * to last 3 sts, k3 in Cardinal (B). Continue working Fence for another 23 (23, 23, 23, 23, 23, 21, 21, 21, 21, 21, 21) rows. Break off Cardinal (B) and Parchment (C) and join in Saxe (D). Work 37 (41, 41, 45, 45, 49, 25, 25, 25, 25, 25, 25) rows.

NEXT ROW: Cast off 5 (5, 5, 6, 6, 6, 5, 5, 5, 5, 5, 5) sts purlwise, purl to end. Decrease at neck edge only by k2tog or p2tog on the next 4 (4, 5, 5, 6, 7, 6, 6, 7, 7, 8, 8) rows, then decrease at neck edge on alternate rows until 23 (25, 27, 30, 32, 33, 21, 23, 24, 26, 27, 29) sts. remain. Work straight until Front measures the same as the Back to the shoulder shapings.

NEXT ROW: With right side facing, cast off 8 (8, 9, 10, 11, 11, 7, 8, 8, 9, 9, 10) sts, knit to end of row. NEXT ROW: purl. Repeat the last two rows once more.

NEXT ROW: cast off remaining 7 (9, 9, 10, 10, 10, 7, 7, 8, 8, 9, 9) sts.

RIGHT FRONT

Work as for Left Front but working buttonhole as follows: Work 2 rows in Twisted Rib. NEXT ROW: rib 2, cast off 2 sts, rib to end. NEXT ROW: Rib to last 4 sts, cast on 2 st (over cast off sts), rib 2.

Continue in rib as for Left Front. On last row increase 2 sts evenly along, leaving the last 6 sts on a safety pin for the Band: 35 (38, 41, 44, 47, 50, 35, 37, 39, 41, 43, 45) sts. Continue as for Left Front until you reach the Fence. NEXT ROW: *k3 in Cardinal (B), k1 in Parchment (C), repeat from * to end of row (as before). Complete Fence, change to Saxe (D) and complete as Left Front, reversing all shapings.

SLEEVES (Both the same)

Using Saxe (D) and No. 3¼mm (UK 10, US 3) needles for the Child's and No. 5½mm (UK 5, US 8) needles for the Adult's, cast on 37 (39, 41, 43, 45, 47, 26, 28, 28, 28, 30, 30) sts and work Rib as for Back. On the last row increase 14 (14, 14, 14, 14, 14, 11, 11, 11, 11, 11, 11) sts evenly across: 51 (53, 55, 57, 59, 61, 37, 39, 39, 39, 41, 41) sts. Change to No. 4mm (UK 8, US 5) needles for the Child's and No. 6½mm (UK 3, US 10) needles for the Adult's and work in st st, increasing each end of the 5th (5th, 5th, 5th, 5th, 5th, 3rd, 3rd, 3rd, 3rd, 3rd, 3rd) row and following 6th (6th, 6th, 6th, 6th, 6th, 4th, 4th, 4th, 4th, 4th, 4th) rows until 73 (75, 79, 83, 87, 101, 65, 69, 71, 71, 73, 73) sts. Continue until sleeve measures 12 (14, 15, 16, 17, 18, 19, 19, 19, 19, 20, 20)in, 30 (36, 38, 41, 43, 46, 48, 48, 48, 48, 51, 51)cm or the length required.
Cast off loosely.

LEFT BAND

Transfer the 6 sts from the safety pin on to No. 3¼mm (UK 10, US 3) needles for the Child's and No. 5½mm (UK 5, US 8) for the Adult's and work in Twisted Rib, changing colours accordingly until Band reaches the neck when slightly stretched, leave on a safety pin and sew band on to Left Front by oversewing into place.

RIGHT BAND
(Buttonhole Band)

Place 8 (8, 8, 8, 8, 10, 10, 10, 10, 10, 10, 10) sewing pins equally spaced down Left Band, including one opposite the buttonhole in the Rib and allowing one, three rows after the neckband has been started. Work as for Left Band working the

buttonholes in the appropriate places, as before in the Rib. When Band is complete with 7 (7, 7, 7, 7, 7, 9, 9, 9, 9, 9, 9) buttonholes and measures the same as the Left Band, sew in place.

NECKBAND

With right sides together, sew shoulder seams together with a fine back stitch. Using Saxe (D) and No. 3¼mm (UK 10, US 3) needles for the Child's and No. 5½mm (UK 5, US 8) needles for the Adult's, rib 6 from Band, pick up and k28 (28, 30, 32, 32, 34, 26, 26, 26, 26, 26, 26) sts up side of neck, k24 (26, 28, 28, 30, 36, 28, 28, 30, 30, 32, 32) sts across Back, pick up and k28 (28, 30, 32, 32, 34, 26, 26, 26, 26, 26, 26) sts up other side of neck, rib 6 from Band: 92 (94, 100, 104, 106, 116, 92, 92, 94, 94, 96, 96) sts. Work 3 rows in rib. NEXT ROW (Buttonhole Row): Rib 2, cast off 2 sts, rib to end.
NEXT ROW: Rib to last 4 sts, cast on

2 sts, rib 2. Work 4 (4, 4, 4, 4, 4, 2, 2, 2, 2, 2, 2) more rows in rib. Cast off loosely.

EMBROIDERY
(as indicated in diagrams)

Trace the diagram of the cat on to tracing paper and cut out. Place the wrong side of the pattern on the reverse of the white fur fabric and cut out, using pointed scissors, being careful to cut the backing only and not the fur. Cut out another cat with the pattern the right way up on the reverse of the black fur fabric in the same way. Cut out the patch on the cat's tummy (B) and transfer the white piece to the black cat and the black piece to the white cat. Secure 2 – 12mm safety cat's eyes through each cat's face. Place the 15mm noses, black on the white cat and pink on the black cat, and secure in place. Embroider the mouths with black and white yarn respectively and back stitch. Push three black and white whiskers respectively either side of each

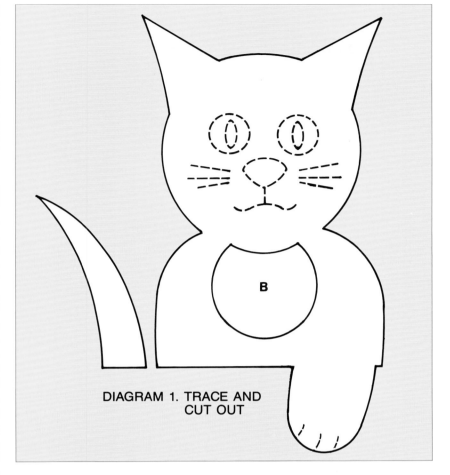

DIAGRAM 1. TRACE AND CUT OUT

mouth and sew securely in place with black or white cotton. Thread the bell on the red ribbon and sew securely round each cat's neck. Oversew both cats to the top of the Fence, placing some stuffing behind the heads. Embroider the paws and divide for the leg, using black on the white cat and white on the black cat. Embroider the flowers on the grass (see Diagram 2) using a large chain stitch for the petals, filled in with satin stitch. Work one in Royal, Yellow and Red, with alternate french knots in the centres. Using stem stitch, embroider the stems with Dark Green, work leaves in a large chain stitch and fill in with satin stitch. On the Adult cardigan place 3 embroidery stones in the centre of each flower instead of working a french knot (if desired). On the Sleeves, embroider using Yellow, and chain stitch a wavy line up the centre and then using Red and chain stitch, embroider two petals in each curve (see Diagram 3). Sew the buttons

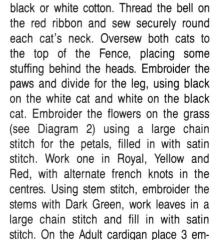

in place opposite the buttonholes.

FINISHING

Press as the instructions on the ball band, avoiding the attachments. With a fine back stitch sew in the sleeves, sew up the side seams and the sleeve seams, oversewing the ribbing. Sew on the buttons opposite the buttonholes. Follow the washing instructions on the ball band, but do not tumble dry if safety eyes and noses have been used.

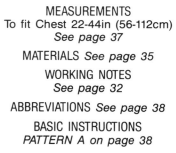

---

7   THE FROGS**

MEASUREMENTS
To fit Chest 22-44in (56-112cm)
See page 37

MATERIALS *See page 35*

WORKING NOTES
See page 32

ABBREVIATIONS *See page 38*

BASIC INSTRUCTIONS
PATTERN A on page 38

FRONT

Using Indian Yellow (A), cast on the required number of sts as in PATTERN A and work Rib. Change to No. 4mm (UK 8, US 5) needles and work in st st beginning with a knit row for 2 (6, 16, 16, 22, 28, 56, 54, 54, 54, 54, 54) rows. Work Chart 1 as follows, joining in colours where necessary:
ROW 1: k17 (20, 23, 26, 29, 32, 35, 38, 41, 44, 47, 50) sts, work 1st row of chart, k17 (20, 23, 26, 29, 32, 35, 38, 41, 44, 47, 50) sts.
ROW 2: p17 (20, 23, 26, 29, 32, 35, 38, 41, 44, 47, 50) sts, work 2nd row of chart, p17 (20, 23, 26, 29, 32, 35, 38, 41, 44, 47, 50) sts. Continue until chart is completed.

Work a further 5 (9, 9, 13, 13, 17, 17, 19, 19, 21, 21, 21) rows.
DIVIDE FOR THE NECK: Follow PATTERN A.

BACK

Using Indian Yellow (A) follow PATTERN A.

SLEEVES (Both the same)

Using Cherry (D) follow PATTERN A for Rib. Change to No. 4mm (UK 8, US 5) needles and follow PATTERN A. AT THE SAME TIME, when 4 rows have been worked for all sizes from the Rib, work Chart 2, placing the 13 sts central in the Sleeve. When chart is complete, work 6 rows st st in Cherry (D). Repeat Chart 2 and the 6 rows until Sleeve measures the required length, finishing with Cherry (D) at the top.

NECKBAND

Using Indian Yellow (A) follow PATTERN A.
Darn in all loose ends from the motifs.

EMBROIDER
(as indicated on the chart)

Using White (E) embroider the lines for the legs, divides and the toadstool divide with a back stitch. Using Cherry (D) embroider the noses and sides of mouth with a back stitch and embroider the mouths with a chain stitch. Embroider the frogs' eyes as in the diagram in the section on Embroidery, using White (E), Black and Indian Yellow (A).

FINISHING

Follow PATTERN A.

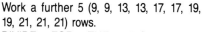

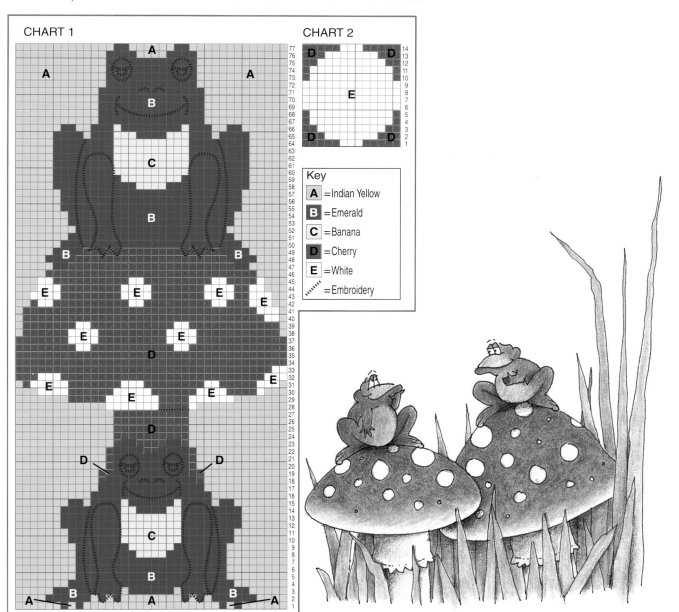

MEASUREMENTS
To fit Chest 22-44in (56-112cm)
See page 37

MATERIALS *See page 35*

WORKING NOTES
See page 32

ABBREVIATIONS
See page 38

BASIC INSTRUCTIONS
PATTERN A on page 38

FRONT

Using White (A), cast on the required number of sts as in PATTERN A and work Rib. Change to No. 4mm (UK 8, US 5) needles and work in st st beginning with a knit row for 2 (6, 16, 16, 22, 28, 56, 54, 54, 54, 54, 54) rows. Work Chart 1 as follows, joining in colours where necessary:
ROW 1: k1 (4, 7, 10, 13, 16, 19, 22, 25, 28, 31, 34) sts, work 1st row of chart, k1 (4, 7, 10, 13, 16, 19, 22, 25, 28, 31, 34) sts.
ROW 2: p1 (4, 7, 10, 13, 16, 19, 22, 25, 28, 31, 34) sts, work 2nd row of chart, p1 (4, 7, 10, 13, 16, 19, 22, 25, 28, 31, 34) sts.

NOTE that in Rows 22 and 23 the Rib of Jed's jumper is worked in Rib: *k1, p1, repeat from * 6 times. At the beginning of row 51, break off White (A) and join in Turquoise (K). Continue until chart is completed. Work a further 2 (6, 6, 10, 10, 14, 14, 16, 16, 18, 18, 18) rows.
DIVIDE FOR THE NECK: Follow PATTERN A.

BACK

Using White (A) work as for Front omitting the teddies but changing to Turquoise (K) at the same place. Complete as in PATTERN A.

SLEEVES (Both the same)

Using White (A) follow PATTERN A. AT THE SAME TIME when 38 (38, 38, 38, 38, 48, 60, 60, 60, 60, 60, 60) rows have been worked, break off White (A), join in Turquoise (K) and work Chart 2, placing the 44 sts central in the Sleeve. When Chart 2 is complete, continue until Sleeve measures the required length.

NECKBAND

Using Turquoise (K) follow PATTERN A. Darn in all loose ends from motifs.

SCARVES

Using No. 3¼mm (UK 10, US 3) needles and Guard's Red (G) cast on 5 sts and work in garter stitch (every row knit) until scarf measures 4in (10cm). Cast off. Make another scarf in Corona Yellow (J). Make a fringe one end of each scarf and sew one round each teddy's neck in position as on chart.

BACK OF HEAD (TWO)

With No. 4mm (UK 8, US 5) needles and Dark Chocolate (E), cast on 16 sts and work in st st for 22 rows, cast off. Make another one using Majestic Mink (F).

EMBROIDERY
(as indicated on the chart)

Attach two 15mm safety eyes to both teddies' faces as indicated in Working Notes or embroider them using White (A) and Black (B) yarn, as shown in the section on Embroidery. Embroider the girl teddy's nose with Majestic Mink (F) in satin stitch and using back stitch embroider the mouth. Embroider Jed's nose and mouth with Black (B). Using Majestic Mink (F) and back stitch, embroider the divide and the paws where they hold hands. Using Royal (H) embroider round the Ark on Jed's jumper with back stitch. Using White, embroider the lines on the sweaters and the divide on the trousers. Make a pom-pom (see page 33) using Guard's Red (G) and sew securely to top of hat. Using the red ribbon make a bow and sew securely to the teddy's head. Sew two pieces of the 39mm Ship Ahoy Red ribbon for the skirt as indicated on the chart, overlapping the two pieces, oversewing in place.

FINISHING

Follow PATTERN A.

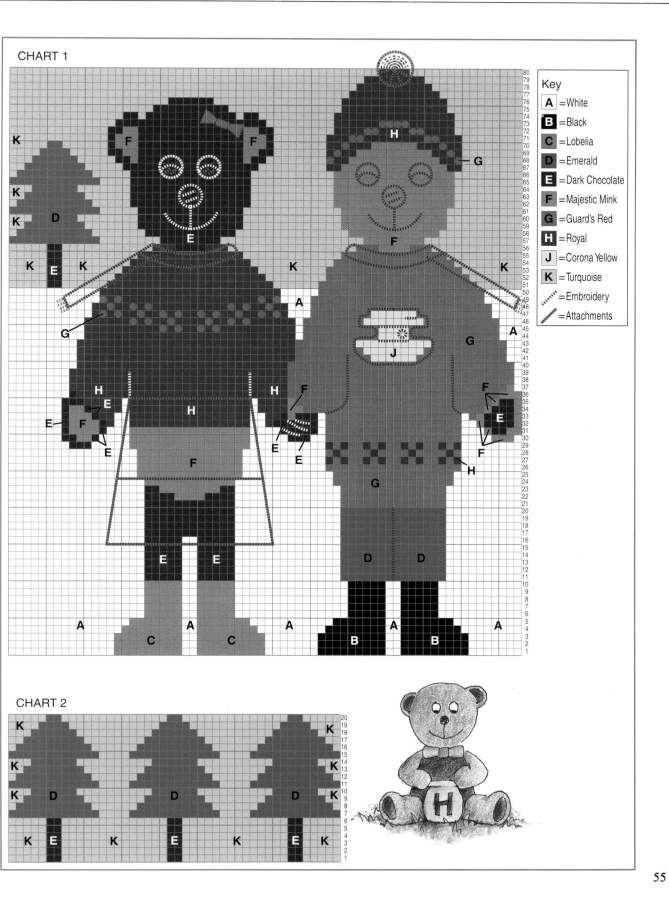

CHART 1

Key
- **A** = White
- **B** = Black
- **C** = Lobelia
- **D** = Emerald
- **E** = Dark Chocolate
- **F** = Majestic Mink
- **G** = Guard's Red
- **H** = Royal
- **J** = Corona Yellow
- **K** = Turquoise
- ⋮ = Embroidery
- ▨ = Attachments

CHART 2

MEASUREMENTS
To fit Chest 22-44in (56-112cm)
See page 37

MATERIALS
See page 35

WORKING NOTES
See page 32

ABBREVIATIONS
See page 38

BASIC INSTRUCTIONS
PATTERN A on page 38 and
PATTERN B on page 39

FRONT

Using Peacock Blue (A), cast on the required number of sts as in PATTERN B and work Rib. Change to No. 4mm (UK 8, US 5) needles and Silver Blue (B) and work in st st beginning with a knit row for 14 (16, 30, 30, 38, 50, 70, 70, 72, 72, 72, 72) rows. Work chart as follows, joining in colours where necessary:
ROW 1: k7 (10, 13, 16, 19, 24, 27, 30, 33, 36, 39, 42) sts, work 1st row of chart, k7 (10, 13, 16, 19, 24, 27, 30, 33, 36, 39, 42) sts.
ROW 2: p7 (10, 13, 16, 19, 24, 27, 30, 33, 36, 39, 42) sts, work 2nd row of chart, p7 (10, 13, 16, 19, 24, 27, 30, 33, 36, 39, 42)

sts. Continue working from chart, changing the background colour to Hydrangea Blue (E) at the beginning of Row 39. When chart is complete work a further 4 (8, 8, 12, 12, 16, 16, 18, 18, 20, 20, 20) rows.
DIVIDE FOR THE NECK: Follow PATTERN B.

BACK

Work as for Front omitting the Penguins, but changing to Hydrangea Blue (E) at the same place. Complete as in PATTERN B.

SLEEVES (Both the same)

Using Peacock Blue (A) work Twisted Rib as in PATTERN A. Change to Hydrangea Blue (E) and using No. 4mm (UK 8, US 5) needles, work in st st as follows:
1st ROW: k21 (22, 23, 24, 25, 26, 27, 28, 28, 29, 29, 30) sts in Hydrangea Blue (E), k9 in Imperial Purple (G), k21 (22, 23, 24, 25, 26, 27, 28, 28, 29, 29, 30) sts in Hydrangea Blue (E).
Continue working Sleeve, increasing as in PATTERN A and AT THE SAME TIME, working blocks of colour in the centre as follows: 8 rows (including 1st Row) of

Imperial Purple (G), 8 rows of Peacock Blue (A), 8 rows of Veridian (Green) (H), 8 rows of Citron (Yellow) (F), 8 rows of Cherry (J). Repeat the colour sequence up the Sleeve. When Sleeve measures the required length (ending with a block of 8 rows of colour in centre) cast off loosely.

NECKBAND

Follow PATTERN B for instructions, using Hydrangea Blue (E) to pick up sts, then work colour sequence as follows:
Sizes 22-30in (56-76cm):
ROW 1: Using Imperial Purple (G), purl.
ROW 2: Rib.
ROW 3: Using Peacock Blue (A), purl.
ROW 4: Rib.
ROW 5: Using Citron (F), purl.
ROW 6: Rib.
ROW 7: Using Cherry (J), purl.
ROW 8: Rib.
ROW 9: Using Cherry (J), knit (hemline).
ROW 10: Rib.
ROW 11: Using Citron (F), purl.
ROW 12: Rib.
ROW 13: Using Peacock Blue (A), purl.
ROW 14: Rib.
ROW 15: Using Imperial Purple (G), purl.
ROW 16: Rib.
Cast off loosely with a No. 4mm (UK 8, US 5) needle.
For sizes 32-44in (81-112cm):
Follow the above instructions but work two extra rows of Veridian (H) after the Peacock Blue (A) before and after the hemline.

SCARVES

Using No. 3¼mm (UK 10, US 3) needles and Imperial Purple (G), cast on 4 sts.
1st ROW: Purl. 2nd – 6th ROWS: Knit. Repeat 6 rows of garter st in stripes as follows: Peacock Blue (A), Veridian (H), Citron (F), Cherry (J), Imperial Purple (G), Peacock Blue (A), Veridian (H), Citron (F), and Cherry (J). Cast off. Make a fringe of Veridian to go on the bottom. Make a second scarf the same way.
Darn in all loose ends from motifs.

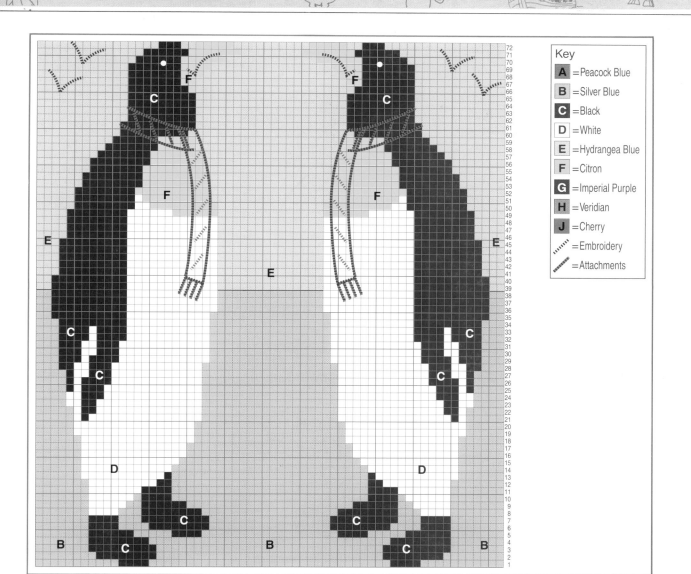

Key

A	=Peacock Blue
B	=Silver Blue
C	=Black
D	=White
E	=Hydrangea Blue
F	=Citron
G	=Imperial Purple
H	=Veridian
J	=Cherry
	=Embroidery
	=Attachments

EMBROIDERY
(as indicated on the chart)

Using Black (C), embroider the beaks using back stitch and embroider 4 birds in the sky. Using White (D), embroider an eye on each penguin. Sew a scarf round each penguin's neck.

FINISHING

Follow PATTERN A.

MEASUREMENTS
To fit Chest 22-44in (56-112cm)
See page 37
MATERIALS *See page 35*
WORKING NOTES *See page 32*
ABBREVIATIONS *See page 38*
BASIC INSTRUCTIONS
PATTERN A on page 38

FRONT

Using Magenta Flame (A), cast on the required number of sts as in PATTERN A. Work Rib as follows (for all sizes):
Work 3 rows Rib (as PATTERN A) in Magenta Flame (A).
NEXT ROW: Using Lobelia (B), purl. NEXT 2 ROWS: rib. NEXT ROW: Using Emerald (C), knit. NEXT 2 ROWS: rib. NEXT ROW: Using Corona Yellow (D), purl. NEXT 2 ROWS: rib. NEXT ROW: Using Guard's Red (E), knit. NEXT 2 ROWS: rib. NEXT ROW: Using Tropical Green (F), purl, increasing 5 sts (for all sizes) evenly along: 70 (76, 82, 88, 94, 100, 106, 112, 118, 124, 130, 136) sts. Change to No. 4mm (UK 8, US 5) needles and work in st st, beginning with a knit

row for 0 (4, 14, 14, 20, 26, 54, 52, 52, 52, 52, 52) rows. Work Chart 1 as follows, joining in colours where necessary:
ROW 1: k2 (5, 8, 11, 14, 17, 20, 23, 26, 29, 32, 35) sts, work 1st row of chart, k1 (4, 7, 10, 13, 16, 19, 22, 25, 28, 31, 34) sts.
ROW 2: p1 (4, 7, 10, 13, 16, 19, 22, 25, 28, 31, 34) sts, work 2nd row of chart, p2 (5, 8, 11, 14, 17, 20, 23, 26, 29, 32, 35) sts. Continue until Chart 1 is completed changing from Tropical Green (F) to Stormcloud (K) at the beginning of Row 47. Work a further 2 (6, 6, 10, 10, 14, 14, 16, 16, 18, 18, 18) rows.
DIVIDE FOR THE NECK: Follow PATTERN A.

BACK

Work Rib as for Front. Purl 1 row in Tropical Green (F) increasing 5 sts evenly along for all sizes. Change to No. 4mm (UK 8, US 5) needles and work in st st for 10 (14, 24, 24, 30, 36, 64, 62, 62, 62, 62, 62) rows. Work Chart 2 as follows, joining in colours where necessary:
ROW 1: k3 (6, 9, 12, 15, 18, 21, 24, 27, 30, 33, 36) sts, work 1st row of chart, k2 (5, 8, 11, 14, 17, 20, 23, 26, 29, 32, 35) sts.
ROW 2: p2 (5, 8, 11, 14, 17, 20, 23, 26, 29,

32, 35) sts, work 2nd row of chart, p3 (6, 9, 12, 15, 18, 21, 24, 27, 30, 33, 36) sts. Continue until Chart 2 is completed. Work a further 16 rows for all sizes and then change from Tropical Green (F) to Stormcloud (K). Complete Back as in PATTERN A.

RIGHT SLEEVE

Using Magenta Flame (A) follow PATTERN A for required number of sts and work Rib as for Front. NEXT ROW: using Tropical Green (F), purl, increasing the appropriate number of sts according to PATTERN A. Change to No. 4mm (UK 8, US 5) needles and follow PATTERN A. AT THE SAME TIME when 2 (4, 10, 10, 10, 10, 10, 14, 14, 14, 14, 14) rows have been worked place Chart 1(A) — the Rabbit (17 sts) central in the Sleeve. When the chart is complete, work a further 12 rows for all sizes. Break off Tropical Green (F) and join in Stormcloud (K). Work 5 rainbow stripes (20 sts) up the centre of the Sleeve as follows: count your sts, take away 21, divide the number by 2, knit that number in Stormcloud (K), k4 sts Magenta Flame (A), k4 sts Lobelia (B), k4 sts Emerald (C), k4 sts Corona Yellow (D), k4 sts Guard's Red (E), knit in Stormcloud (K) to the end of the row. Use separate balls of yarn for each stripe, twisting one colour over the next.
Note: There is 1 more st in Stormcloud (K) after the rainbow, than before.
Continue until Sleeve measures the required length.

LEFT SLEEVE

Work Rib as for Right Sleeve, increasing on the purl row. Change to No. 4mm (UK 8, US 5) needles and follow PATTERN A. AT THE SAME TIME when 8 (10, 16, 16, 16, 16, 16, 20, 20, 20, 20, 20) rows have been worked, place Chart 3 in the centre of the Sleeve. When Chart 3 is complete, continue until Tropical Green (F) measures the same as the right Sleeve before changing colour. Break off Tropical Green (F) and join in Stormcloud (K) and work rainbow in centre as before, but reversing

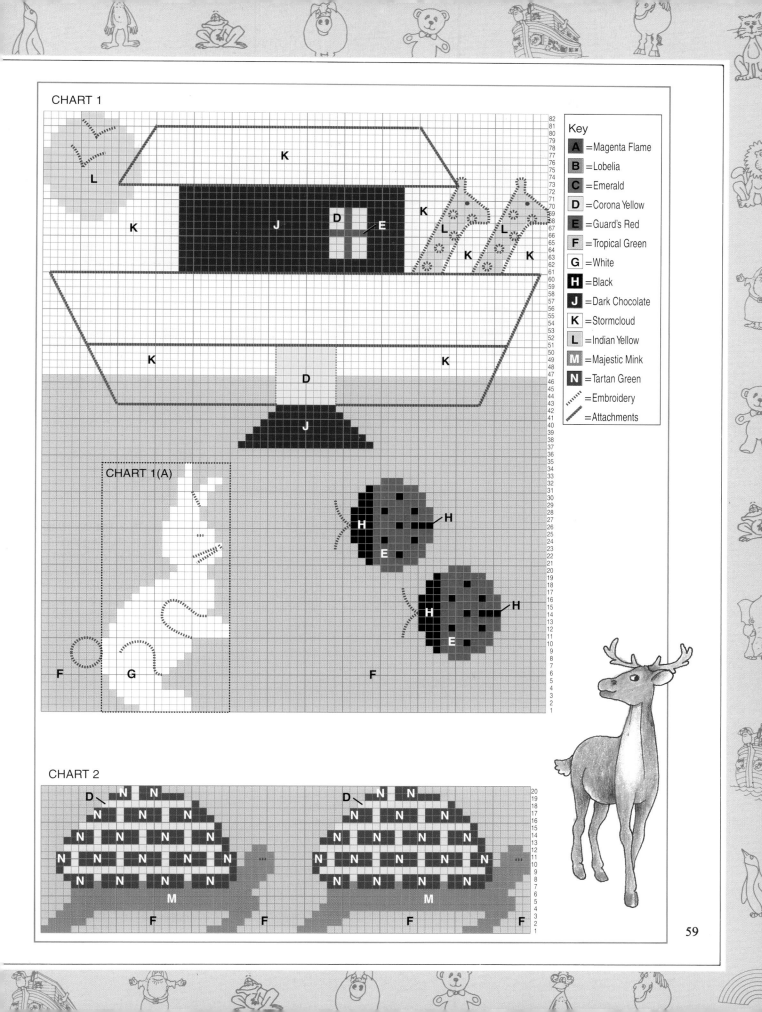

CHART 1

CHART 1(A)

CHART 2

Key
A = Magenta Flame
B = Lobelia
C = Emerald
D = Corona Yellow
E = Guard's Red
F = Tropical Green
G = White
H = Black
J = Dark Chocolate
K = Stormcloud
L = Indian Yellow
M = Majestic Mink
N = Tartan Green
= Embroidery
= Attachments

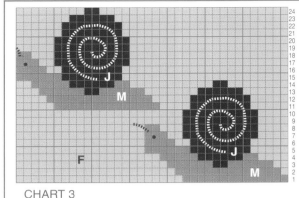

Key

F = Tropical Green
J = Dark Chocolate
M = Majestic Mink
╌╌╌ = Embroidery

CHART 3

Rib. NEXT ROW: Cast off loosely. Darn in all loose ends from motifs.

EMBROIDERY
(as indicated on the chart)

Using Majestic Mink (M) and back stitch, outline the giraffes, work an eye and some spots in satin stitch on the giraffes. Embroider the whiskers, eye and lines on the rabbits and also the lines on the snails. Using Black (H) and back stitch, embroider two birds in the sky, the antennae on the ladybirds, the eyes on the tortoises and the antennae and eyes on the snails. Sew a pom-pom on to each rabbit for their tails. Sew, with small oversewing sts, the 39mm Red Ship Ahoy ribbon on to the sweater for the Ark, the lower ribbon either side of the entrance and the upper ribbon overlapping the lower one. Sew one piece across the top of the Ark for the roof, sloping all the sides.

FINISHING

Follow PATTERN A.

the colours, ie. Guard's Red (E), Corona Yellow (D), Emerald (C), Lobelia (B) and Magenta Flame (A). Continue until Sleeve measures the required length.

NECKBAND

Using Stormcloud (K) follow PATTERN A. Work all sizes as follows:
NEXT ROW: Using Magenta Flame (A), purl. NEXT ROW: Rib. NEXT ROW: Using Lobelia (B), purl. NEXT ROW: Rib. NEXT ROW: Using Emerald (C), purl. NEXT ROW: Rib. NEXT ROW: Using Corona Yellow (D), purl. NEXT ROW: Rib. NEXT ROW: Using Guard's Red (E), purl. NEXT ROW: Rib. NEXT ROW (hemline): knit. NEXT ROW: Rib. NEXT ROW: Using Corona Yellow (D), purl. NEXT ROW: Rib. NEXT ROW: Using Emerald (C), purl. NEXT ROW: Rib. NEXT ROW: Using Lobelia (B), purl. NEXT ROW: Rib. NEXT ROW: Using Magenta Flame (A), purl. NEXT ROW:

---

11   INSIDE THE ARK***

MEASUREMENTS
To fit Chest 24-44in (61-112cm)
See page 37

MATERIALS
See page 36

WORKING NOTES
See page 32

ABBREVIATIONS
See page 38

BASIC INSTRUCTIONS
PATTERN A on page 38

FRONT

(NOTE: the first size is a 24in (61cm) before the brackets.) Using Guard's Red (A), cast on the required number of sts as in PATTERN A and work Rib increasing 5 sts evenly along the last row: 76 (82, 88, 94, 100, 106, 112, 118, 124, 130, 136)

sts. Change to No. 4mm (UK 8, US 5) needles and work in st st as follows, breaking off Guard's Red (A).

1st ROW: Using Emerald (B) k36 (39, 42, 45, 48, 51, 54, 57, 60, 63, 66) sts, join in Black (C), k4 sts for all sizes, join in Corona Yellow (D), k36 (39, 42, 45, 48, 51, 54, 57, 60, 63, 66) sts.

This is the 1st Row of the Lower Box instructions.

NOTE: Each chart has to be centred in each box but they don't start on the same line. For each size the box has the following number of rows: 41 (46, 46, 49, 52, 66, 66, 66, 66, 66, 66). I suggest for each pair of motifs you write the number of rows on a piece of paper and mark off where each one starts. Keeping the 4 sts Black (C) in the centre, work each box as follows; the chart may begin on a purl row, depending on the size.

LOWER RIGHT-FACING BOX
(Background colour Emerald (B))

Work 9 (11, 11, 12, 14, 21, 21, 21, 21, 21, 21) rows. Work Chart 4 as follows: work 4 (6, 7, 9, 10, 12, 13, 15, 16, 18, 19) sts, work 1st row of chart, work to end. Continue until chart is complete. Work a further 8 (11, 11, 13, 14, 21, 21, 21, 21, 21, 21) rows.

LOWER LEFT-FACING BOX
(Background colour Corona Yellow (D))

Work 1 (4, 4, 5, 7, 14, 14, 14, 14, 14, 14) rows. Work Chart 3 as follows: work 9 (10, 12, 13, 15, 16, 18, 19, 21, 22, 24) sts, work 1st row of chart, work to end. Continue until chart is complete. Work a further 1 (3, 3, 5, 6, 13, 13, 13, 13, 13, 13) rows.

Break off all colours. Using Black (C) work 5 rows. Continue in st st as follows:

NEXT ROW (Sizes 24in (61cm) and 30in (76cm) only): Using Guard's Red (A) k36 (45) sts, join in Black (C), work 4 sts, join in Royal Blue (E) and k36 (45) sts. This is the 1st row of the Upper Box Instructions.

ALL OTHER SIZES: Using Royal Blue (E), p– (39, 42, –, 48, 51, 54, 57, 60, 63, 66) sts, join in Black (C), work 4 sts, join in Guard's Red (A), p– (39, 42,

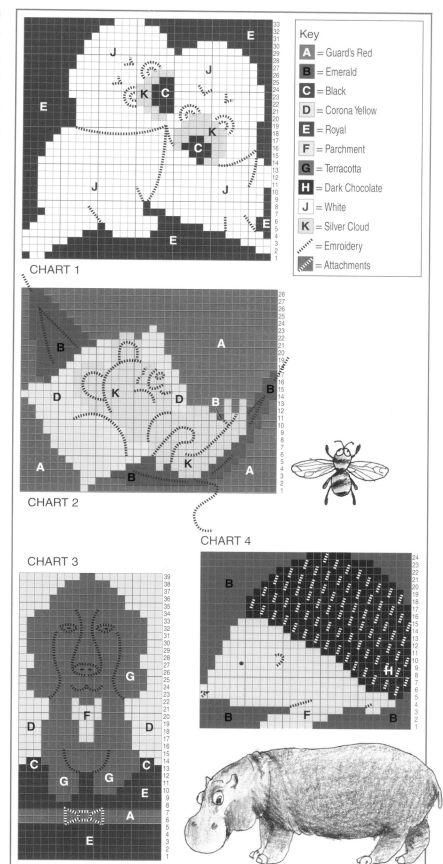

Key

A	= Guard's Red
B	= Emerald
C	= Black
D	= Corona Yellow
E	= Royal
F	= Parchment
G	= Terracotta
H	= Dark Chocolate
J	= White
K	= Silver Cloud
	= Emroidery
	= Attachments

CHART 1

CHART 2

CHART 4

CHART 3

61

-, 48, 51, 54, 57, 60, 63, 66) sts. This is the 1st Row of the Upper Box Instructions.

Keeping the 4 sts Black (C) in centre, work each box as follows:

UPPER RIGHT-FACING BOX
(Background colour Guard's Red (A))

Work 7 (9, 9, 11, 12, 19, 19, 19, 19, 19, 19) rows. Work Chart 2 as follows: work 1 (3, 4, 6, 7, 9, 10, 12, 13, 15, 16) sts, work 1st row of chart, work to end. Continue until chart is complete. Work a further 6 (9, 9, 10, 12, 19, 19, 19, 19, 19, 19) rows.

UPPER LEFT-FACING BOX
(Background colour Royal Blue (E))

Work 4 (7, 7, 8, 10, 17, 17, 17, 17, 17, 17) rows. Work Chart 1 as follows: work 1 (3, 4, 6, 7, 9, 10, 12, 13, 15, 16) sts, work 1st row of chart, work to end. Continue until chart is complete. Work a further 4 (6, 6, 8, 9, 16, 16, 16, 16, 16, 16) rows. Break off all colours. Using Black (C) work 5 rows.

NEXT ROW: Using Corona Yellow (D), k36 (39, 42, 45, 48, 51, 54, 57, 60, 63, 66) sts, join in Black (C) and k4 sts, join in Emerald (B) and k36 (39, 42, 45, 48, 51, 54, 57, 60, 63, 66) sts. Work 1 (1, 3, 3, 7, 7, 9, 9, 11, 11, 11) more rows ending with right side facing.
DIVIDE FOR THE NECK: Follow PATTERN A.

BACK

Work exactly as for Front. When Back measures the same as the Front to the shoulder shapings, follow PATTERN A.

SLEEVES
(Both the same)

Using Guard's Red (A) follow PATTERN A for rib. NEXT ROW: change to No. 4mm (UK 8, US 5) needles, break off Guard's Red (A) and join in Emerald (B), knit to centre 4 sts, join in Black (C) and k4, join in Corona Yellow (D) and work to end of row.
NOTE: If you want your Sleeves shorter or longer than stated measurement, work

fewer or more rows before and after the horizontal Black stripe.
Continue following instructions from PATTERN A and AT THE SAME TIME when work measures $6\frac{1}{2}$ (7, $7\frac{1}{4}$, $7\frac{1}{2}$, $7\frac{1}{2}$, $8\frac{1}{4}$, $8\frac{1}{4}$, $8\frac{1}{4}$, $8\frac{1}{4}$, $8\frac{1}{2}$, $8\frac{1}{2}$)in, 16.5 (18, 18.5, 19, 19, 21, 21, 21, 21, 21.5, 21.5)cm from beginning of st st, finishing with a purl row, break off colours and join in Black (C). Work 5 rows. NEXT ROW: Purl in Royal Blue (E) to centre 4 sts, p4 in Black (C), join in Guard's Red (A) and work to end of row.
Continue until Sleeve measures 14 (15, 16, 17, 18, 18, 19, 19, 19, 20, 20)in, 36 (38, 41, 43, 46, 46, 48, 48, 48, 51, 51)cm or required length. Cast off loosely.

NECKBAND

Using Guard's Red (A) follow PATTERN A.
Darn in all loose ends from the motifs and changes of colour.

EMBROIDERY
(as indicated on charts)

Hedgehog: Using Black (C) embroider eye, nose, ear and leg divides. With Parchment (F), embroider the prickles on his back.
Dog: Using White (J) and back stitch, embroider face and divide for legs. Make a small bow with the red ribbon and sew on to the box.
Mouse: Using Black (C), embroider the face, ears, arm, legs and lines on the hammock. Working a chain stitch, embroider the rope holding the hammock up either end. Using Silver Cloud (K) and back stitch, embroider the mouse's tail.
Seals: Using Silver Cloud (K), embroider the eyes, eyebrows and divides with back stitch. Place a dot with Black (C) in each eye.

FINISHING

Follow PATTERN A.

THE RAINBOW**

MEASUREMENTS
One Size
Child's (actual measurement):
35in (89cm)
Adult's (actual measurement):
52in (132cm)
See page 37

MATERIALS
See page 36

WORKING NOTES
See page 32

ABBREVIATIONS
See page 38

TENSION
Child's (Double Knitting: AS PATTERN A.
Adult's (Mohair): 16 sts and 22 rows measure 4in (10cm) over st st using No. 5½mm (UK 5, US 8) needles (or size needed to obtain this tension).

NOTE: The instructions for this cardigan are given in two sizes, both using the same chart and the same number of sts for the Fronts and Back. The Child's is in Double Knitting, the instructions given first and the Adult's is in Mohair, the instructions given in brackets.

RIGHT FRONT

Using Blue Frost/Silky Blue (A) and No. 3¼mm (UK 10, US 3)/4½mm (UK 7, US 6) needles, cast on 56 (52) sts and work Rib as follows:
1st ROW: *k1, p1, *k1b, p1 repeat from * to end of row.
2nd ROW: As 1st Row.
3rd ROW (buttonhole row): Rib 2, cast off 2 sts, rib to end of row.
4th ROW: Rib 52 (48) sts, cast on 2 sts, rib 2 sts. Continue with Twisted Rib until Rib measures 1½ (2)in, 4 (5)cm. On the last row increase 4 (8) sts evenly along the first 50 (46) sts. Leave the last 6 sts on a safety pin: 54 (54) sts. Change to

No. 4mm (UK 8, US 5)/5½mm (UK 5, US 8) needles and work in st st beginning at Row 1 of Chart 1, joining in separate balls of each colour, including the background colour (A). Continue until Chart 1 is complete, casting off 6 sts at the beginning of Row 109 and then decreasing as shown. After Row 135 is complete, cast off 12 sts at the beginning of the next and alternate rows. Work 1 row. Cast off the remaining 12 sts.

LEFT FRONT

Work Rib as for Right Front omitting the buttonhole in the band. When Rib is complete, work the increase row leaving the first 6 sts on a safety pin and then increasing 4 (8) sts evenly along the 50 (46) sts: 54 (54) sts. Change to No. 4mm (UK 8, US 5)/5½mm (UK 5, US 8) needles, working in st st, work from Chart 2 until complete, casting off 5 sts at the beginning of row 108. After row 134 is complete, cast off 12 sts at the beginning of the next and alternate rows. Work 1 row. Cast off the remaining 12 sts.

BACK

Using Blue Frost/Silky Blue (A) and No. 3¼mm (UK 10, US 3)/4½mm (UK 7, US 6) needles, cast on 100 (92) sts and Rib as for Left Front. On the last row increase 8 (16) sts evenly along: 108 (108) sts. Change to No. 4mm (UK 8, US 5)/5½mm (UK 5, US 8) needles and work in st st. Continue until Back measures the same as the Front to the shoulder shapings. NEXT 6 ROWS: cast off 12 (12) sts at the beginning of each row. Leave the remaining 36 (36) sts on a stitch holder.

RIGHT SLEEVE

Using Blue Frost/Silky Blue (A) and No. 3¼mm (UK 10, US 3)/4½mm (UK 7, US 6) needles, cast on 46 (32) sts and work in Twisted Rib for 1½ (2½)in, 4 (6)cm. On the last row, *for Child's size*, increase 16 sts evenly along: 62 sts.

For Adult's size: *k1, increase in next st, repeat from * to end of row: 48 sts. Change to No. 4mm (UK 8, US 5)/5½mm (UK 5, US 8) needles and work in st st as follows, joining in separate balls of each colour as follows:

1st ROW: k21 (14) sts in (A), k4 in African Violet/Lavender (B), k4 in Pacific Blue/Pacific Blue (C), k4 in Tropical Green/Tropical Green (D), k4 in Wild Honey/Wild Honey (E), k4 in Crimson/Carmine (F), k21 (14) sts in (A). Continue working stripes up centre of Sleeve and AT THE SAME TIME working the increases as follows:

Child's: Increase each end of the 5th and following 6th rows until 100 sts.

Adult's: Increase each end of the 5th and following 6th rows 6 times and then every 4th row until 84 sts.

Both Sizes: work straight until Sleeve measures 17 (20)in 43 (51)cm or the required length. Cast off loosely.

LEFT SLEEVE

Work as for Right Sleeve, but reversing the stripes up the centre, beginning with Crimson/Carmine (F) and ending with African Violet/Lavender (B).

RIGHT BAND
(Buttonhole Band)

Using No. 3¼mm (UK 10, US 3)/4½mm (UK 7, US 6) needles, transfer sts from safety pin to needle and work in Twisted Rib working buttonholes as in Right Front, working 14 (11) rows between each buttonhole until a further 6 (8) buttonholes have been worked. Work 12 (9) more rows

64

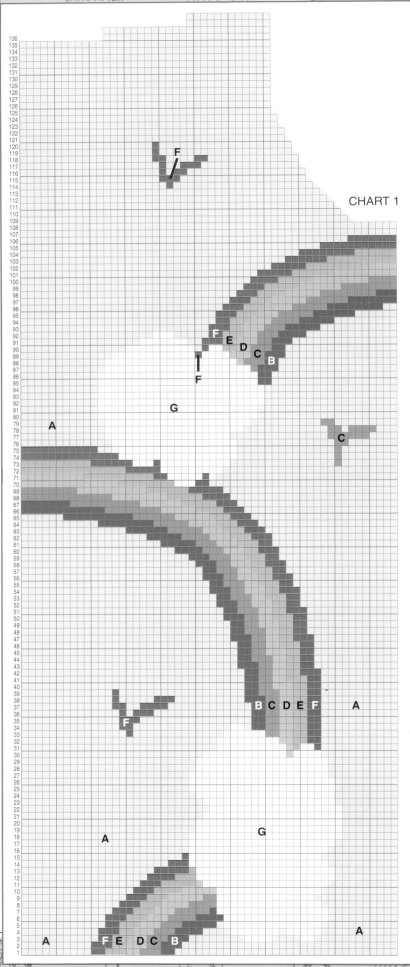

CHART 1

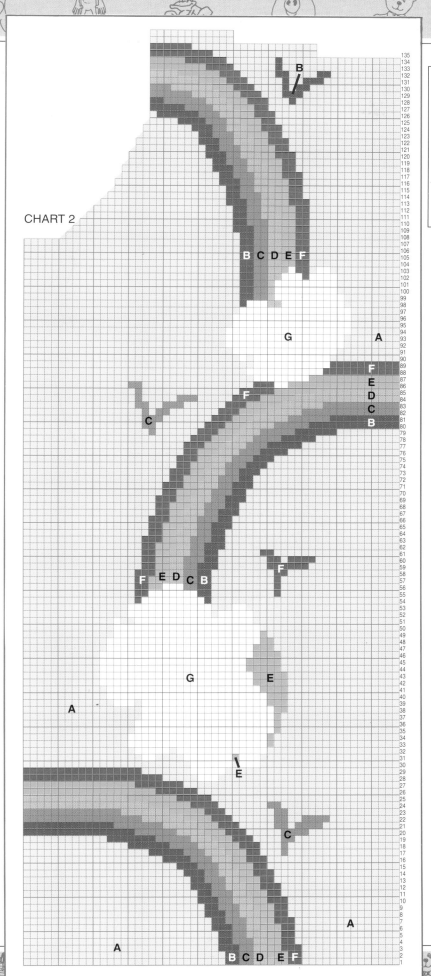

CHART 2

Key

A	= Blue Frost / Silky Blue
B	= African Violet / Lavender
C	= Pacific Blue / Pacific Blue
D	= Tropical Green / Tropical Green
E	= Wild Honey / Wild Honey
F	= Crimson / Carmine
G	= White / White

in Twisted Rib and leave the 6 sts on a safety pin.

LEFT BAND

Work as for the Right Band, omitting the buttonholes, until Band measures the same length, leave the 6 sts on a safety pin.

Sew each band to the Front, stretching into position as necessary. Join the shoulder seams together with fine back stitch.

NECKBAND

Using No. 3¼mm (UK 10, US 3)/4½mm (UK 7, US 6) needles and (A) Rib 6 from Right Band, pick up and knit 36 (28) sts up Right Front, k36 (36) sts from across the Back, pick up and knit 36 (28) sts down Left Front and Rib 6 across Left Band: 120 (104) sts. NEXT ROW: Rib. NEXT ROW: Make a buttonhole as before and Rib to end. NEXT ROW: Rib to last 4 sts, cast on 2 sts, Rib 2. Work a further 4 rows. Cast off loosely.

Darn in all the loose ends from the rainbows, birds and clouds.

FINISHING

Do not press the Child's if the Silky Look is used. Press the Adult's according to the ball band. With a fine back stitch, sew in sleeves, sew up side seams and sleeve seams, oversewing the ribbing. Sew on the buttons opposite the buttonholes. Follow the washing instructions on the ball band. The rainbow buttons are available from: Peapods to Zebras (address in Noah's Address Book on page 71).

BY THE SEASIDE** (Modelled by Jed)

MEASUREMENTS
To fit a 14in (35cm) high Teddy Bear.

ACTUAL MEASUREMENTS
Chest 16in (41cm); Length: 5in (13cm); Sleeve Length: 2in (5cm).

MATERIALS
Small quantity of Sirdar Country Style Double Knitting — about 35g altogether.
(A) Corona Yellow (460)
(B) Lobelia (420)
(C) White (412)
(D) Lupin (429)
(E) Guard's Red (495)
(F) Black (417)
1 pair No. 3¼mm (UK 10, US 3) needles, 1 pair No. 4mm (UK 8, US 5) needles.
2 small buttons.

WORKING NOTES
See page 32

ABBREVIATIONS
See page 38

TENSION
as PATTERN A.

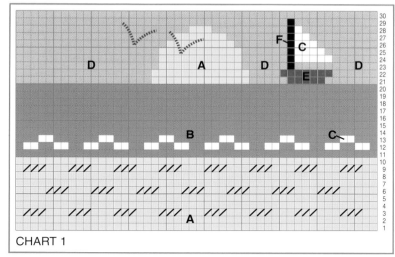

CHART 1

Key
A =Corona Yellow	**E** =Guard's Red
B =Lobelia	**F** =Black
C =White	╱ =Purl on a knit row and knit on a purl row
D =Lupin	⸱⸱⸱⸱ =Embroidery

FRONT

Using Corona Yellow (A) and No. 3¼mm (UK 10, US 3) needles, cast on 44 sts and work 6 rows in Twisted Rib as in PATTERN A. On the last row, increase 4 sts evenly along (48 sts). Change to No. 4mm (UK 8, US 5) needles and work from Chart 1 in st st (unless otherwise stated) until chart is complete. Change to No. 3¼mm (UK 10, US 3) needles and continuing in Lupin (D) work 6 rows in Twisted Rib. Cast off loosely.

BACK

Work Rib as for Front. Change to No. 4mm (UK 8, US 5) needles and st st, work 10 rows in Corona Yellow (A), 10 rows in Lobelia (B), 10 rows in Lupin (D). Change to No. 3¼mm (UK 10, US 3) needles and work 6 rows in Twisted Rib. Cast off loosely.

SLEEVES (Both the same)

Using No. 3¼mm (UK 10, US 3) needles and Corona Yellow (A), cast on 26 sts and work 4 rows in Twisted Rib. On the last row increase 8 sts evenly along (34 sts). Change to No. 4mm (UK 8, US 5) needles and Lupin (D), work in st st for 12 rows. Cast off loosely.

Darn in all the loose ends. Press under a dry cloth, or according to ball band. Embroider two birds in the sky using Black (F).

FINISHING

Sew Back to Front top Ribs together by oversewing for 1in (3cm) from outside towards the centre, both sides on the wrong side. Sew in the Sleeves with a fine back stitch. Sew up the side and Sleeve seams with a fine back stitch. Make two loops either side of the neck for the buttons. Sew the buttons on the back Rib.

PORTRAIT OF JED** (Modelled by JED)

MEASUREMENTS
As 'By the Seaside'.

ACTUAL MEASUREMENTS
As 'By the Seaside'.

MATERIALS
Small quantity of Sirdar Country Style Double Knitting — about 35g altogether
(A) Cream (411) — approx. 30g.
(B) Dark Chocolate (439)
(C) Majestic Mink (482)
Black (417) — embroidery
White (412) — embroidery
2 — 15mm safety goo-goo eyes.
6in (15cm) — 9mm Offray Rainbow Stripe ribbon.
1 pair No. 3¼mm (UK 10, US 3) needles, 1 pair No. 4mm (UK 8, US 5) needles.
2 small buttons.

WORKING NOTES
See page 32

ABBREVIATIONS
See page 38

TENSION
As PATTERN A

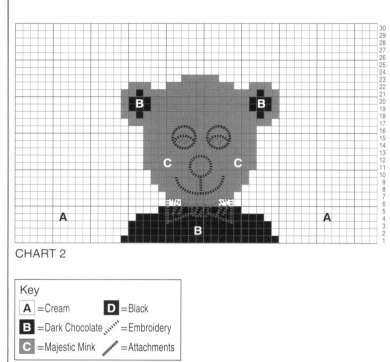

CHART 2

Key
A = Cream   D = Black
B = Dark Chocolate   ······ = Embroidery
C = Majestic Mink   ///// = Attachments

FRONT

Using Cream (A) follow instructions for 'By the Seaside' following Chart 2 and working Neck Rib in Cream (A).

BACK

Using Cream (A) work as for Front omitting the motif.

SLEEVES (Both the same)

Using Cream (A) follow instructions for 'By the Seaside'.
Darn in all the loose ends. Press under a dry cloth, or according to ball band.

FINISHING

Secure the goo-goo eyes to the face (see Working Notes), embroider the nose with satin stitch and the mouth with back stitch using Black (D). Make a bow with the Rainbow ribbon and secure to neck. Complete as 'By the Seaside' sweater.

THE RAINBOW** (Modelled by JED)

MEASUREMENTS
As 'By the Seaside'.

ACTUAL MEASUREMENTS
As 'By the Seaside'.

MATERIALS
Small quantity of Sirdar Country Style Double Knitting — about 35g altogether.
(A) Emerald (479)
(B) Lupin (429)
(C) White (412)
(D) Magenta Flame (430)
(E) Royal (449)
(F) Corona Yellow (460)
(G) Guard's Red (495)
(H) Tartan Green (419)
(J) Dark Chocolate (439)
Black (417) — embroidery
1 pair No. 3¼mm (UK 10, US 3) needles, 1 pair No. 4mm (UK 8, US 5) needles.
2 small buttons.

WORKING NOTES
See page 32

ABBREVIATIONS
See page 38

TENSION
As PATTERN A.

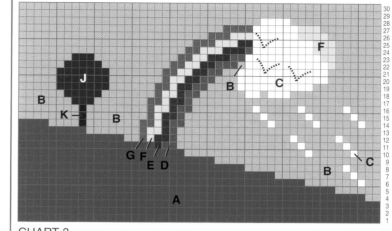

CHART 3

Key
A =Emerald		**G** =Guard's Red	
B =Lupin		**H** =Black	
C =White		**J** =Tartan Green	
D =Magenta Flame		**K** =Dark Chocolate	
E =Royal		⋯⋯ =Embroidery	
F =Corona Yellow			

FRONT

Using Emerald (A) follow instructions for 'By the Seaside' following Chart 3 and working Neck rib in Lupin (B).

BACK

Using Emerald (A) follow instructions for Front working from Chart 3 again but working the 1st row as a purl row and omitting the rain, cloud, sun, rainbow and tree. Work Neck Rib as 'By the Seaside'.

SLEEVES (Both the same)

Using Lupin (B) follow instructions for 'By the Seaside'.
Darn in all loose ends. Press under a dry cloth, or according to ball band.

FINISHING

Using Black (H) embroider three birds on the cloud. Finish as 'By the Seaside'.

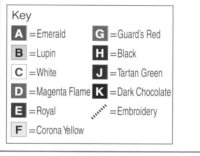

IN THE COUNTRY** (Modelled by JED)

MEASUREMENTS
As 'By the Seaside'.

ACTUAL MEASUREMENTS
As 'By the Seaside'.

MATERIALS
Small quantity of Sirdar Country Style Double Knitting — about 35g altogether.
(A) Emerald (479)
(B) Saxe (440)
(C) Tropical Green (444)
(D) Corona Yellow (460)
(E) Dark Chocolate (439)
(F) Tartan Green (419)
(G) Stormcloud (472)
1 pair No. 3¼mm (UK 10, US 3) needles, 1 pair No. 4mm (UK 8, US 5) needles.
2 small buttons.

WORKING NOTES
See page 32

ABBREVIATIONS
See page 38

TENSION
As PATTERN A.

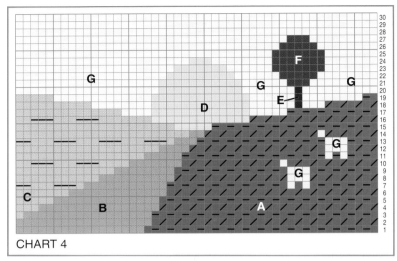

CHART 4

Key
A = Emerald   F = Tartan Green
B = Saxe   G = Stormcloud
C = Tropical Green   — = Purl on knit row / knit on purl row
D = Corona Yellow   / = Knit on purl row
E = Dark Chocolate

FRONT

Using Emerald (A) follow instructions for 'By the Seaside' following Chart 4 and working Neck Rib in Stormcloud (G).

BACK

Using Emerald (A) follow instructions for 'By the Seaside' for Rib. Change to No. 4mm (UK 8, US 5) needles and work in st st for 19 rows. Change to Stormcloud (G) and work a further 11 rows. Change to No. 3¼mm (UK 10, US 3) needles and work Rib. Cast off loosely.

SLEEVES (Both the same)

Using Emerald (A) work Rib as for 'By the Seaside'. Change to No. 4mm (UK 8, US 5) needles and Stormcloud (G) and complete sleeve. Darn in all the loose ends.

FINISHING

Follow the instructions for 'By the Seaside'.

Noah's Address Book

NAME	ADDRESS	NOTES
Sirdar plc (UK)	Flanshaw Lane, Alverthorpe, Wakefield, West Yorkshire, WF2 9ND.	Write to Sirdar if you have difficulty obtaining the yarn.
Knitting Fever Incorporated (USA)	180 Babylon Turnpike, Roosevelt, NY 11575, USA.	The agent for Sirdar Yarn in the USA. Write to Knitting Fever Incorporated if you have difficulty obtaining the yarn.
Diamond Yarn (Canada) Corp	9697 St. Lawrence Boulevard, Montreal PQ, Canada.	The agent for Sirdar yarn in Canada.
Doris Design Agentur GmbH	Ispingrader Street 43, 5608 Radevomwald, Germany.	The agent for Sirdar yarn in Germany.
Alliance Knitting Yarns	Factory Road, Private Bag 50032, Mosgiel, Nr. Dunedin, New Zealand.	The agent for Sirdar yarn in New Zealand.
C. M. Offray Ltd & Son	Fir Tree House, Church Road, Ashford, Middlesex, TW15 2PH.	All the ribbon used in this book was supplied by Offray.
Peapods to Zebras	4 The Crescent, Hyde Park Corner, Leeds, LS6 2NW. Tel: (0532) 742044.	The Elephant, Pig and Rainbow buttons are available from this address.
Mo Smith	c/o Autumn House, Alma Park, Grantham, Lincs., NG31 9SL. (MAIL ORDER ONLY).	Knitting kits for a selection of sweaters from this book are available by mail order. Please send SAE for price list. The safety eyes, ribbon, etc., are also available from Mo, if you are unable to purchase any of the attachments from your local haberdashery or wool shop.
JED	c/o Mo Smith, Autumn House, Alma Park, Grantham, Lincs., NG31 9SL.	Jed is looking for someone to adopt him. He is 14″ tall, was created by Mo and made by Merrythought Ltd. His hobbies include sliding through rainbows and wearing hand-knitted sweaters. Jed costs £17.75 plus £1.50 for p & p (UK price) and all the profits go to ACET (AIDS Care, Education and Training).

AUTUMN HOUSE

GRANTHAM ENGLAND